FUNDAMENTALS OF MATH

BOOK 2

ALGEBRA I

Sequel
(More Problems)

by

Jerry Ortner

AuthorHouse™
1663 Liberty Drive
Bloomington, IN 47403
www.authorhouse.com
Phone: 1-800-839-8640

© 2011 Jerry Ortner. All rights reserved.

No part of this book may be reproduced, stored in a retrieval system, or transmitted by any means without the written permission of the author.

First published by AuthorHouse 4/22/2011

ISBN: 978-1-4567-4054-2 (sc)
ISBN: 978-1-4567-4055-9 (e)

Library of Congress Control Number: 2011902846

Printed in the United States of America

Any people depicted in stock imagery provided by Thinkstock are models, and such images are being used for illustrative purposes only. Certain stock imagery © Thinkstock.

This book is printed on acid-free paper.

Because of the dynamic nature of the Internet, any web addresses or links contained in this book may have changed since publication and may no longer be valid. The views expressed in this work are solely those of the author and do not necessarily reflect the views of the publisher, and the publisher hereby disclaims any responsibility for them.

TABLE OF CONTENTS

Lesson numbers refer to the lessons in Algebra I, Second Edition.

LESSON 1 – Algebraic Operations of Signed Numbers

Simplify.

1. $0 - 9$

2. $13 + (-5)$

3. $8 - 5$

4. $(9)(-4)(-2)$

5. $\dfrac{72}{-8}$

6. $-35 + 12$

7. $(-16) - (-22)$

8. $2 - 7$

9. $(-4)(-9)$

10. $8 + (-23) - 17$

11. $14 + (-12) + (-8)$

12. $6 + (-8)$

13. $(-9) + (-7)$

14. $\dfrac{24}{-6}$

15. $(-18) + (-100)$

16. $5 - 5$

17. $(12)(-8)$

18. $(-40) + 79$

19. $6 + (-5) + (-8) + 12$

20. $-3 - 5$

21. $-14 + (-33)$

22. $26 + (-4)$

23. $(-8)(-5)$

24. $9 - 5$

25. $(-8) - (-10) + 23$

26. $\dfrac{42}{-3}$

27. $(9)(-2)(3)$

28. $3 - 6$

29. $6 + (-1) - 7$

30. $(-3)(7) - 16$

31. $\dfrac{-18}{-3}$

32. $(7)(-9)$

33. $(-8) + 6 + (-2)$

34. $6 - (-10)$

35. $\dfrac{36}{-4} + (-5)$

36. $(-5) + (-8) + 23$

3

37. $(10) + (-23) - 5$

38. $8(-4)$

39. $3 - (-8)$

40. $\dfrac{60}{3(4)}$

41. $(5)(-4)(3)$

42. $(-4) + (-6) + (-10)$

43. $\dfrac{64}{(4)(-8)}$

44. $-2 - (-8)$

45. $12 + 9 - (6) + 2$

46. $(1)(2)(3)(-4)$

47. $\dfrac{(5)(4)}{(2)(2)}$

48. $16 - 8 + (-3)$

49. $\dfrac{-100}{5 \cdot 2}$

50. $8 - 16$

51. $(-16) + (-5) + 4$

52. $\dfrac{-48}{-6}$

53. $(17)(-3)$

54. $(-3) - (-5) + 4$

55. $(6)(-1)(-4)$

56. $\dfrac{18}{(3)(-3)}$

57. $(-1)(-3)(-5)(-2)$

58. $(8)(-7)(-2)$

59. $25 + (50) - 40$

60. $(-8) + (-16) - 6$

61. $\dfrac{54}{-6}$

62. $(14)(-1)(2)$

63. $(-8) - (-7) + 6$

64. $9 + \dfrac{18}{3}$

65. $-2 - (-6)$

66. $\dfrac{-48}{(-3)(2)(2)}$

67. $(-7) - (-8)$

68. $42 + (-7)(6)$

69. $\dfrac{27}{(-3)(3)}$

70. $6 + (-5) - 9$

LESSON 3 – Removal of Brackets/Parentheses
(PEMDAS)

Simplify.

1. $6(4 + 9)$

2. $(4)(6)(2 \cdot 3)$

3. $\dfrac{4(9 + 4) + 8}{3(6 - 4)}$

4. $-(-8) - 3(8 - 7)$

5. $-(4 - 6) + 5[4 + (-7)]$

6. $\dfrac{(-6)(4)}{(2)(6) - (6 + 4)}$

7. $7(2 \cdot 3 + 6)$

8. $4(2 + 4 - 7)$

9. $-(2) \div (8 - 6)$

10. $[6 \cdot (2)] + 5(4 - 1)$

11. $4 - 2 + 4(5)$

12. $7(3 - 5) + 20$

13. $8 + \dfrac{18}{2} - 6$

14. $\dfrac{(3 - 1)(5 - 7) + 20}{4 + (-6)}$

15. $-8(-4 + 2) + 5$

16. $2 + 7 - 8$

17. $12 - 3 \cdot 6$

18. $8 \div 4 + 2$

19. $5 + (6 - 3)$

20. $(7 + 3) - (4 + 3)$

21. $16 - 8 + (4 - 6)$

22. $(9 + 3) \times 4 - 5(7 - 2)$

23. $[24 - (8 \cdot 20)] \times 2$

24. $8 \times (7 - 5) + 6$

25. $[-12 + (-18)] \div 5$

26. $(-8 + 10) + (15 - 7)$

27. $5 \times (2 + 3) \div 5$

28. $5 + 3 \cdot 4 - 7$

29. $(-6) + 2 \cdot 8 - 5$

30. $12 \cdot 2 - 8 \cdot (-3)$

LESSON 4 – Evaluate a Square Root, Cube Root, and Absolute Value

Simplify.

1. $\sqrt[3]{64} + \sqrt[3]{8}$

2. $(\sqrt{81})(\sqrt{64})$

3. $-(\sqrt{36}) + |{-10}|$

4. $(\sqrt[3]{27})(\sqrt{25})$

5. $|{-17}| + |32|$

6. $\sqrt{8^2} - \sqrt[3]{125}$

7. $(\sqrt[3]{1000})(\sqrt{25})$

8. $-(\sqrt{49})(\sqrt[3]{8})$

9. $|6 + 4 - 18| \, (\sqrt[3]{216})$

10. $(\sqrt{64}) \cdot \frac{1}{2}(\sqrt[3]{64})$

11. $|{-10}|^2 - 5^2 - \sqrt{49}$

12. $(\sqrt[3]{343})(\sqrt{9}) + \sqrt{16}$

13. $-(\sqrt{100}) + \sqrt[3]{8} + \sqrt[3]{125}$

14. $\sqrt[3]{729} + \sqrt{81} + 4^2$

15. $7^2 + \sqrt{49} + |{-7}|$

16. $|{-12}| + |10| + 5^2 - (-5)^2$

17. $-(\sqrt{49}) + \sqrt[3]{512} - \sqrt{81}$

18. $(\sqrt{16} + \sqrt[3]{64})^2 - (6)^2$

19. $3^2 - \sqrt{81} - \sqrt[3]{8}$

20. $|{-12}| + |12| + 5^2 + (-5)^2$

LESSON 5 – Left to Right Inside Parentheses with Numerous Signs

Simplify.

1. $8 + 6 - 4 \div 2 \cdot 5$

2. $-17 + 23 \cdot 2 - 8$

3. $25 \div 5 \cdot 4 + 8 \cdot 2$

4. $8(7) + 27 \div 3 - 10$

5. $19 + 9 \cdot 2 - 40 + 3$

6. $-16 \div 4 + 8 \cdot 6 - 20$

7. $\dfrac{14}{2} \cdot 9 - 8 \cdot 7 + 13$

8. $-42 \div 7 + 6 - 13 \cdot 3$

9. $16 - \dfrac{8}{2} + 4 \times 3 - 28$

10. $\dfrac{9 + 36 \div 4 - \dfrac{27}{3}}{4 + 5 - 6}$

11. $(8 + \dfrac{6}{3} - 9) \cdot 7$

12. $\left(14 + \dfrac{28}{7}\right) - \left(\dfrac{18 - 12}{2}\right)$

13. $\left[(6 + 5) - \dfrac{4}{2}\right] \cdot 8$

14. $\dfrac{16 + (-32)}{4} + \dfrac{9 - 5}{2}$

15. $\dfrac{(6 \cdot 9)}{2} - \left[\dfrac{(6 + 4)}{5} \cdot 18\right]$

LESSON 6 – Evaluating Exponents with a Negative Base and Signed Numbers

Simplify.

1. $(-3)^2 + (2)^4$

2. $3^3 + (-2)^2$

3. $(-4)^3 - (5^2)$

4. $(-8)^2 + 64$

5. $(-6)^2 + (-5)^2$

6. $(-3)^3 + (4)^2$

7. $10^2 + (-10)^2$

8. $(-\sqrt[3]{64})(\sqrt[3]{27})$

9. $(-6)^2 \cdot \sqrt[3]{125}$

10. $(-8)^2 + (-\sqrt[3]{27})$

11. $(-5)^2 + 2^2 - (-4)^2$

12. $(|-10|)(|-3|) + 1^3$

13. $-4^2 - (-3)^2$

14. $4^2 - (-3)^2$

15. $\sqrt{16} + |-3 + 7 + 4|$

16. $(-10)^2 - (-10^2)$

17. $(-8)^2 + \sqrt[3]{125}$

18. $(-4)^2 - (-3^2)$

19. $8^2 + (-9)^2$

20. $-(-10^2) + (-10)^2$

LESSON 7 – Simple Mathematical Equations
using Addition and Subtraction Rules

Solve for "N".

1. $18 - N = 12$

2. $N + 8 = 32$

3. $9 - N = -41$

4. $N + 12 = 47$

5. $8 + N = 27$

6. $64 - N = 83$

7. $N - 23 = 15$

8. $72 - N = 47$

9. $N + 16 = -8$

10. $12 - N = -23$

11. $N + 10 = 13$

12. $5 - N = 25$

13. $N - 12 = 16$

14. $23 - N = -37$

15. $5 + N = 12$

16. $32 - N = 63$

17. $N + 16 = 12$

18. $47 + N = 22$

19. $N - 12 = 41$

20. $55 - N = 66$

LESSON 8 – Simple Mathematical Equations
using Division and Multiplication Rules

Solve for "x".

1. $5x = 35$

2. $\dfrac{42}{x} = 3$

3. $64 = 4x$

4. $12x = 132$

5. $\dfrac{x}{4} = 21$

6. $-8x = 48$

7. $\dfrac{10}{-x} = 2$

8. $3x = -18$

9. $\dfrac{x}{5} = 17$

10. $9x = -36$

11. $\dfrac{x}{2} = -8$

12. $7x = 84$

13. $\dfrac{48}{x} = -16$

14. $6x = -54$

15. $\dfrac{x}{3} = 27$

16. $4x = -84$

17. $64 = \dfrac{x}{8}$

18. $-3x = 12$

19. $5x = 65$

20. $\dfrac{x}{10} = -7$

LESSON 9 – Solving Equations with Several Rules

Example 1: $6x + 5 = 23$

Solution:

$$
\begin{array}{rrrl}
6x & + & 5 & = & 23 \\
\text{Step 1} & & -\ 5 & & -\ 5 & \text{Subtraction 5 from both sides.}
\end{array}
$$

$$
\begin{array}{rrl}
6x & = & 18 \\
\text{Step 2} \qquad \dfrac{6x}{6} & = & \dfrac{18}{6} & \text{Divide both sides by 6.} \\
x & = & 3
\end{array}
$$

Example 2: $\dfrac{x}{3} - 4 = 8$

Solution:

$$
\begin{array}{rrrl}
\dfrac{x}{3} & - & 4 & = & 8 \\
\text{Step 1} & & +\ 4 & & +\ 4 & \text{Add 4 to both sides.}
\end{array}
$$

$$
\begin{array}{rrl}
\dfrac{x}{3} & = & 8 \\
\text{Step 2} \qquad \dfrac{3x}{3} & = & 12(3) & \text{Multiply both sides by 3.} \\
x & = & 36
\end{array}
$$

Example 3: $4x + 6x - 8 = 22 + 30$

Solution:

Step 1 $10x\ -\ 8\ =\ 52$ Combine like terms on both sides.
Step 2 $\ +\ 8\ =\ +\ 8$ Add 8 to both sides.

$$
\begin{array}{rrl}
10x & = & 60 \\
\text{Step 3} \qquad \dfrac{10x}{10} & = & \dfrac{60}{10} & \text{Divide both sides by 10.} \\
x & = & 6
\end{array}
$$

Solve for "x". Round to the nearest hundredth where necessary.

1. $2x + 7 = 15$

2. $26 - 3x = 17$

3. $3x + 2x - 7 = 18$

4. $36 = 4x + 8$

5. $3x + 12 = 7x + 84$

6. $22 - 7x = 6x - 119.5$

7. $\frac{3}{4}x + 1\frac{1}{2}x = 7.25 + 3.1$

8. $4.8x + 1.5x = 52.4$

9. $62 + 7x = 12x - 23$

10. $3x + 5x - 10 = 4x + 17 + 21$

11. $12 = 5x - 7$

12. $\frac{x}{4} - 6 = 9$

13. $3x + 24 = 7x - 36$

14. $2\frac{1}{2}x + 12 = 1\frac{3}{4}x - 12$

15. $5x - 30 = 2x + 12$

16. $7.5x + 15x = 100 + \frac{70}{2}$

17. $32 - 5x = 7x - 40$

18. $4x - 10 = 5x - 18$

19. $8\frac{3}{4}x = 5\frac{1}{3}x + 17\frac{1}{12}$

20. $-6x - 12 = 7x + 27$

21. $2x + 5 - 4x = 16 + 2x + 13$

22. $12 - 7x + 3 = -2x + 5$

23. $14 + 5x + 3x = 6x - 26$

24. $12x = 32 - 4x$

25. $3x + 27 = 7x - 1$

26. $2x + 5 = 7x + 45$

27. $36 - 7x = 2x - 9$

28. $6x - 5 = 5(x + 1)$

29. $4x + 4 = 5x + 16$

30. $5x - 3 = -2(4 - 3x)$

31. $-3x - 15 = 2x$

32. $2(x + 1) = 3(x + 2)$

33. $2x - 5 = 7x + 30$

34. $4(x + 2) = 2(x - 4)$

35. $8x = 5x + 21$

36. $2x - (1 + x) = 13$

37. $2(x - 7) = 42 - 2x$

38. $3x + 4 = 2(x + 5)$

39. $6x - 2 = 4x + 2$

40. $4x - 5 + 3 = 7 - 2x$

41. $4 - (3x + 6) = -11$

42. $25 + 7x - 1 = 4x$

43. $(5x + 1) + (3x - 2) = -17$

44. $10x - 5 + 12 = 7x + 21 - 4x$

45. $2x - 8 - (x - 12) = 11$

46. $5 - 4x = x + 20$

47. $4 + 3(x + 2) + 11 = 33$

48. $5x + 7 - 2x = 11$

49. $3x + 2x - 5 = 13 - 2(x + 2)$

50. $5x + 2 - x = 22$

51. $x + 15 + 3x = -1$

52. $5x - (3 + x) = -31$

53. $4(x - 3) + 3x = 16$

54. $8 + 4(x + 11) = 16$

55. $(5x - 1) - (3x - 2) = -17$

56. $x + 6 + 3x - 4 = 14$

57. $3(x - 2) - 2 = 5(x + 3) - 7(x - 1)$

58. $7(x + 2) = 5(x + 4)$

59. $-2(x + 3) = 4$

60. $8x - 9 + x - 17 = 3x + 4 + 8x - 12$

LESSON 12 – Solve Decimal Equations

Example 1: $1.4x + 6 = -22$

 Solution: Multiply all three terms by 10.

$$1.4x(10) + 6(10) = (-22)(10)$$
$$14x + 60 = -220 \quad \text{Subtract 60 from both sides.}$$
$$14x = -280 \quad \text{Divide by sides by 14.}$$
$$x = -20$$

Check it out: $1.4(-20) + 6 = -22$
$$-28 + 6 = -22$$
$$-22 \overset{\checkmark}{=} -22 \quad \text{AOK!}$$

Note: Students sometime like to get variables and constants on opposite sides of the equation. It is your choice. See Example 3.

Example 2: $2.4x + 0.6x = 50.46 + 12.3$

 Solution: I suggest adding 2.4x and 0.6x on the left side. Also, adding 50.46 and 12.3 on the right side.

$$3x = 62.76 \quad \text{Divide both sides by 3.}$$
$$x = 20.92$$

Check it out: $2.4(20.92) + 0.6(20.92) = 50.46 + 12.3$
$$50.208 + 12.552 = 62.76$$
$$62.76 \overset{\checkmark}{=} 62.76 \quad \text{AOK!}$$

Example 2: $4.75x + 16.4 = 2.50x - 88.1$

Solution:

4.75x	+	16.4	=	2.50x	−	88.1
-2.50x				2.50x			Subtract 2.50x from both sides.
2.25x	+	16.4	=		−	88.1
	−	16.4			−	16.4	Subtract 16.4 from both sides.
2.25x			=		−	104.5

$$\frac{2.25x}{2.25} = -\frac{104.5}{2.25} \quad \text{Divide both sides by 2.25.}$$
$$x = -42$$

Solve for "x". Round to the nearest hundredth where necessary.

1. $2.5x + 3 = -26 + 13$

2. $0.4 - 1.2x = 4.0$

3. $1.4x = 0.49 - 0.7x$

4. $5.5x + 67.94 + 2.3x = 31.7 + 0.36$

5. $0.6x - 1.4 = 1$

6. $\dfrac{x}{-4.5} = 0.6$

7. $8(x + 0.5) = -12$

8. $-2.4x + 3.75 = 3.2x - 17.306$

9. $1.2x - 3.6 + 0.3x = 2.4$

10. $0.5 - 1.5x = 3.5$

11. $14.6 + 6.3x = 2.55x - 5.275$

12. $2.5x + 0.75 = 0.5x$

13. $1.4x - 7 = 5 - 0.6x$

14. $\dfrac{0.2x}{8} = 4.32$

15. $-6.4x + 3.1 = 1.6x + 19.9$

16. $3.45x - 13.27 = -5.64x + 43.997$

17. $0.5x + 2x - 7 = 3.4 - 0.4$

18. $-33.2 = -18.2 + 5x$

19. $4.8x - 16.25 = 5.45x + 14.5$

20. $3.7x = 4.5x - 10 - 5.8x$

15

LESSON 13 – Solving Fractional Equations

Solve for the unknown.

1. $\dfrac{x}{2} + 1 = x - 5$

2. $\dfrac{4x}{3} - \dfrac{16}{5} = 2\dfrac{2}{5}$

3. $\dfrac{2}{3}(4x - 1) - \dfrac{3}{5}(x + 1) = \dfrac{1}{2}$

4. $\dfrac{x}{3} = x - 2$

5. $\dfrac{5x}{6} - 12 = \dfrac{2x}{3} - 7$

6. $x + 2 = \dfrac{x}{3} - 4$

7. $\dfrac{3(x + 1)}{5} = 15$

8. $\dfrac{3x - 1}{4} = 2$

9. $6\left(x - \dfrac{1}{2}\right) = \dfrac{9}{2}$

10. $\dfrac{x}{6} + \dfrac{3x}{8} = \dfrac{5x}{8} - 5\dfrac{1}{4}$

11. $\dfrac{5x}{2} + \dfrac{2}{3} = \dfrac{3x}{2} + \dfrac{5}{8}$

12. $\dfrac{x}{2} + \dfrac{x}{3} - \dfrac{x}{4} = -35$

13. $8\left(x + \dfrac{1}{8}\right) = 33$

14. $\dfrac{x}{3} + 6\dfrac{1}{6} = -1\dfrac{5}{6} + 2$

15. $\dfrac{5x}{8} - \dfrac{x}{3} = \dfrac{5x}{6} - 13$

16. $-\left(x - \dfrac{1}{2}\right) = 2$

17. $4\dfrac{1}{4} + \dfrac{x}{2} - 3\dfrac{3}{8} = \dfrac{-3x}{4} + 2\dfrac{7}{8}$

18. $\dfrac{2}{3}x - 15 = \dfrac{4}{3}x + 9$

19. $\dfrac{17}{4} + \dfrac{3x}{8} = \dfrac{4x}{5}$

20. $2\dfrac{1}{2}x - x - \dfrac{1}{2} = \dfrac{1}{4}$

21. $6(N - 3) + 4N = 24 - 12$

22. $5.8N + 2\frac{3}{5}N = 21.9 + 41.94$

23. $13N - 4(N - 3) = 21$

24. $65 = 5(N - 9) + 10$

25. $x + (x - 2) = 14$

26. $8N + 15N - 62 = 30$

27. $3.5(x + 4) - 8 = 2(x + 7.5)$

28. $7N + 16 - 4N = 2(N + 4)$

29. $3\frac{2}{3}x + \frac{5}{6}x = 18 + 13.5$

30. $3(N - 12) + 16 = 7$

31. $3(x + 5) - 12 = x + 7$

32. $2.6(x - 5) = -0.4x + 12$

33. $27 - 2(x + 5) = -\frac{3}{2}(x + 10)$

34. $\frac{5}{2}(x + 6) = 4x - 9$

35. $7.4x - 23 = 5\frac{3}{5}x + 13$

36. $\frac{N}{4}(16) + 12 = 2(N - 10)$

37. $2\frac{5}{8}N + \frac{13}{2} = N + 32.5$

38. $4x + 16 = 6x - 4$

39. $5(N - 7) + 2(N - 2) = 0$

40. $\frac{3}{2}(x + 4) - \frac{2}{3}(x - 3) = -2$

41. $2\frac{3}{4}N + 3.6 = 1\frac{2}{3}N + 19.85$

42. $5\frac{1}{2}x + 16 = 3\frac{3}{5}x - 60$

43. $1.76A + 3 - 0.60A = 10(\frac{1}{2}) + 0.32$

44. $\frac{4}{3}B + \frac{5}{8}B - 20.3 = 73.7$

45. $5(2m + 3) - (1 - 2m) = 2[3(3 + 2m) - (3 - m)]$

LESSON 15 – Literal Equations

When solving a literal equation, letters replace most numbers. It can become tricky, so review the examples prior to tackling the practice problems.

Example 1:   Solve $\boxed{V = lwh}$ for "h".

Solution:

Step 1:   Isolate the "h" to one side of the equation and move any coefficients to the opposite side. In $V = lwh$, the coefficients of "h" are "l" and "w". Therefore, divide **_both_** sides of the original equation by lw. You then have:

$$\frac{V}{lw} = \frac{lwh}{lw}$$

Step 2:   Cancel the "lw" on the right side.

Step 3:   Final answer: $\frac{V}{lw} = h$

Example 2:   Solve $\boxed{A = \frac{1}{2}bh}$ for "b".

Solution:

Step 1:   Divide both sides by the coefficient of "b". That would be $\frac{1}{2}h$.

$$\frac{A}{\frac{1}{2}h} = \frac{\frac{1}{2}bh}{\frac{1}{2}h}$$

Step 2:   On the right side of the equation, the $\frac{1}{2}h$ in the numerator and the denominator cancel out.

Step 3:   Final answer: $\frac{A}{\frac{1}{2}h} = b$

18

Example 3:   Solve $\boxed{A = \dfrac{t-4}{r+s}}$ for "r".

Solution:

Step 1:   Multiply both sides by "r + s".

$$A(r+s) = t - 4$$
$$Ar + As = t - 4$$

Step 2:   Subtract "As" from both sides.

$$Ar = t - 4 - As$$

Step 3:   Divide both sides by "A".

$$\frac{Ar}{A} = \frac{t-4-As}{A}$$

Step 4:   Final answer: $r = \dfrac{t-4-As}{A}$

Example 4:   Solve $\boxed{A = p + prt}$ for "r".

Solution:

Step 1:   Subtract "p" from both sides of the equation.

$$A - p = (p - p) + prt$$
$$A - p = prt$$

Step 2:   Divide by the coefficient of "r", which is "pt".

$$\frac{A-p}{pt} = \frac{prt}{pt}$$

Step 3:   Remove the "pt" from the numerator and denominator on the right.

Step 4:   Final answer: $\dfrac{A-p}{pt} = r$

DO NOT TRY TO CANCEL THE "p's" ON THE LEFT!!
THAT'S A BIG NO-NO!

Solve for the indicated variable.

1. Solve for "r": $i = prt$

2. Solve for "b": $A = \frac{1}{2}bh$

3. Solve for "H": $V = LWH$

4. Solve for "L": $A = LW$

5. Solve for "c": $c + g = s$

6. Solve for "h": $V = \frac{bh}{3}$

7. Solve for "g": $V = v - gt$

8. Solve for "r": $A = p + prt$

9. Solve for "L": $P = 2L + 2W$

10. Solve for "h": $S = 2\pi rh + 2\pi r^2$

11. Solve for "n": $s = 180n - 360$

12. Solve for "A": $16A = p^2$

13. Solve for "d": $L = (n - 1)d + a$

14. Solve for "v": $P = Fv$

15. Solve for "I": $E = IR + Ir$

16. Solve for "B": $A + B = 90$

17. Solve for "s": $A = s^2$

18. Solve for "S": $N = \frac{12S}{dtt}$

19. Solve for "p": $A = i + p$

20. Solve for "D": $DR = dr$

21. Solve for "R": $P - QR = TOP$

22. Solve for "W": $3H + \frac{2}{3}W = 5H - 9$

23. Solve for "x": $y(1 + x) = z - y$

24. Solve for "b": $abc = d(1 - ac)$

LESSON 18 – Linear Equations in Two Variables

1. Complete the table of ordered pairs given the equation $4x + 5y = 17$.

	x	y
a.	$\frac{1}{2}$	
b.		2
c.	3	
d.		4

2. Complete the table of ordered pairs given the equation $3y - 2x = -12$.

	x	y
a.		1
b.	2	
c.		0
d.	-3	

3. State (yes or no) whether each ordered pair is a solution of the give equation.

a. $2a + 3b = 13$

(5, –1) _____

(11, –3) _____

b. $3x – 4y = 11$

$(\frac{1}{3}, -\frac{5}{2})$ _____

$(-\frac{5}{3}, -4)$ _____

c. $2c^2 – 4d^2 = 4$

(4, –3) _____

(0, –1) _____

d. $3mn = n^2$

(–3, –9) _____

$(\frac{1}{6}, -\frac{1}{2})$ _____

LESSON 20 – Graphing a Linear Equation

Put **A**x + **B**y = **C** into the form **B**y = –**A**x + **C** and solve for y:

$$y = -\frac{Ax}{B} + \frac{C}{B}$$

where the coefficient of x is the slope (m) and the constant is the y-intercept (b). This gives us the slope-intercept form of the equation:

$$y = mx + b$$

Example 1: Graph the equation 2x + 5y = 16.

Solution:

Step 1:   Solve for y.
Step 2:   Draw a grid.
Step 3:   Locate the y-intercept (b = $\frac{16}{5}$).

Step 4:   Play with the slope (m). "m" means $\frac{\Delta y}{\Delta x}$ or $\frac{\text{change in y}}{\text{change in x}}$. In this example, m = $-\frac{2}{5}$. For every –2 units on the y-axis there is a +5 units movement on the x-axis. Now you have located another point on the grid. Two points determine a line. Connect the points with a line and you have drawn the graph of that linear equation. Extend the line with rays from the two endpoints. Remember: a ray by definition is part of a line with one endpoint.

2x + 5y = 16

Subtract 2x from both sides.

5y = –2x + 16

Divide by 5.

y = $-\frac{2}{5}$x + $\frac{16}{5}$

m = $-\frac{2}{5}$ and b = $\frac{16}{5}$

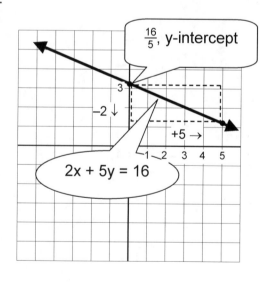

$\frac{16}{5}$, y-intercept

2x + 5y = 16

22

Example 2:   Graph the two equations, $\begin{cases} \mathbf{x - y = 3} \\ 2x + 3y = 8 \end{cases}$, on the **same** grid.

Solution:

x – y = 3
y = x – 3
m = 1 and b = –3
2x + 3y = 8
3y = –2x + 8
$y = -\frac{2}{3}x + \frac{8}{3}$
$m = -\frac{2}{3}$ and $b = \frac{8}{3}$

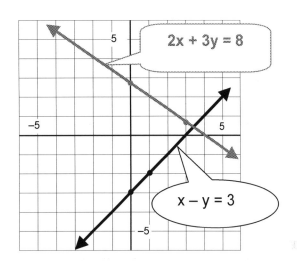

Example 3:   Graph the two equations, $\begin{cases} 2x - y = 5 \\ y - x = -3 \end{cases}$, on the **same** grid.

Solution:

2x – y = 5
y = 2x – 5
m = 2 and b = –5
y – x = –3
y = x – 3
m = 1 and b = –3

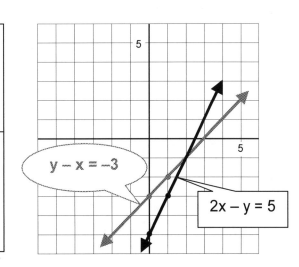

Graph the equations on the same grid. Are these pairs of lines parallel, perpendicular, intersect but not perpendicular, or coincide?

1. $2x + 5y = 4$
   $4x + 10y = 1$

2. $-4x + 3y = 4$
   $-8x + 6y = 0$

3. $8x - 9y = 6$
   $8x + 6y = -5$

4. $3x - 2y = 6$
   $2x + 3y = 3$

5. $y = 2x - 3$
   $2y = -2x + 4$

6. $-5x + 6y = 12$
   $-10x = -12y$

7. $5x - 3y = -2$
   $3x - 5y = -8$

8. $2x - 4y = 12$
   $x - 2y = 6$

9. $5x + 3y = 2$
   $3x - 5y = -1$

10. $3x = 4y$
    $-6x - 12y = 0$

11. $4x - 3y = 10$
    $8x - 6y = 16$

12. $\frac{x}{2} - 3y = 7$
    $2x - 12y = 28$

LESSON 21 – Finding the Slope of a Line Given Two Points

The slope (m) of a line needs refinement.

$$m = \frac{\text{change in y}}{\text{change in x}} \quad \text{or} \quad \frac{\Delta y}{\Delta x} = \frac{y_2 - y_1}{x_2 - x_1}$$

Let's look at this situation in a different way. Suppose you are given two points on a line, (2, 6) and (7, 15), what is the slope of the line?

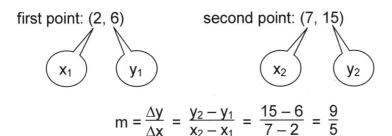

first point: (2, 6)   second point: (7, 15)

x_1 y_1 x_2 y_2

$$m = \frac{\Delta y}{\Delta x} = \frac{y_2 - y_1}{x_2 - x_1} = \frac{15 - 6}{7 - 2} = \frac{9}{5}$$

REMEMBER TO SELECT THE SAME POINT FOR ORDER PURPOSES!!

Find the slope of a line give these two points on the line.

1.   (3, 5) and (8, 11)

2.   (−2, 4) and (7, −5)

3.   (4, −6) and (−2, 3)

4.   (−2, −7) and (−4, −1)

5. $(7, \frac{1}{2})$ and $(8, \frac{2}{3})$

6.   (−12, 4) and (13, 9)

7.   (9, 6) and (−5, 2)

8. $(\frac{3}{5}, \frac{3}{4})$ and (7, 8)

9.   (−6, 7) and (−4, 9)

10.   (5, −4) and (7, −2)

11.   (4, −5) and (6, 8)

12.   (−3, 5) and (7, −11)

13.   (−9, 4) and (−5, 0)

14.   (0, 4) and (8, 7)

15.   (−4, −6) and (−3, −5)

16.   (0, 0) and (7, 14)

17.   (8, −6) and (0, 0)

18. $(\frac{2}{5}, \frac{1}{2})$ and $(\frac{7}{5}, −4)$

19.   (5, 8) and (3, 10)

19.   (9, 4) and (3, 8)

LESSON 22 – Find the Intercepts of a Given Line, Its Slope, and Graph the Line

Example 1: Given the $2x + 3y = 12$, find (a) the value of "x" and (b) the value of "y" respectively if one of the ordered pair is zero.

Solution:

(a) When x = 0 and 0 is substituted into the equation $2x + 3y = 12$, we get $2(0) + 3y = 12$. Since $2 \cdot 0 = 0$, what remains is $3y = 12$. By dividing both sides of $3y = 12$ by 3, we arrive at y = 4. This is where the line intersects the y-axis when x = 0. So, when x = 0, y = 4 and the ordered pair is (0, 4).

(b) When y = 0 and 0 is substituted into the equation $2x + 3y = 12$, we get $2x + 3(0) = 12$. Since $3 \cdot 0 = 0$, what remains is $2x = 12$. By dividing both sides of $2x = 12$ by 2, we arrive at x = 6. This is where the line intersects the x-axis when y = 0. So, when y = 0, x = 6 and the ordered pair is (6, 0).

Sometimes these points, (0, y) and (x, 0), are called the _zeros_ of the equation.

Example 2: Given the equation $2x - 3y = 18$, find the zeros of the equation. Using these intercepts, graph the equation.

Solution:

a. When x = 0, substitute 0 for "x": $2(0) - 3y = 18$. This gives us $-3y = 18$. Dividing both sides by –3, we arrive at y = –6. The y-intercept is (0, –6).

b. When y = 0, substitute 0 for "y": $2x - 3(0) = 18$. This gives us $2x = 18$. Dividing both sides by 2, we arrive at x = 9. The x-intercept is (9, 0).

Our two ordered pairs are (0, –6) and (9, 0). Locate the two points on a grid.

We can now graph the line of the equation $2x - 3y = 18$ by connecting the two points.

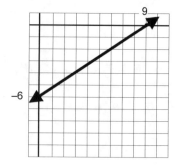

Graph these lines when given the following information. Identify the equation if not given.

1. Given: two points on the line are (1, 4) and (3, 8)

2. Given: two points on the line are (−1, −3) and (4, 2)

3. Given: $3x - 4y = 12$

4. Given: x-intercept is 5, y-intercept is 8. Is the slope positive or negative?

5. Given: $2x + y = 4$

6. Given: lines $x + y = 3$ and $2x - y = 4$. After graphing, are these lines parallel or intersecting?

LESSON 23 – Vertical and Horizontal Lines and "y = mx + b"

What happens when the change in "x" (Δx) or "y" (Δy) is zero? Try these two points:

Example 1:   Find the slope given the points (6, –5) and (–12, –5).

Solution: $m = \dfrac{\Delta y}{\Delta x} = \dfrac{y_2 - y_1}{x_2 - x_1} = \dfrac{-5 - (-5)}{-12 - 6} = \dfrac{-5 + 5}{-18} = \dfrac{0}{-18} = 0$

Our slope is zero. We have a horizontal line that is parallel to the x-axis and the equation of this line is y = –5.

Now let us try these two points:

Example 2:   Find the slope given the points (–8, 6) and (–8, –1).

Solution: $m = \dfrac{\Delta y}{\Delta x} = \dfrac{y_2 - y_1}{x_2 - x_1} = \dfrac{-1 - 6}{-8 - (-8)} = \dfrac{-1 - 6}{-8 + 8} = \dfrac{-7}{0} =$ undefined!

Since we cannot divide by zero, our slope is undefined! We have a vertical line that is parallel to the y-axis and it's equation is x = –8.

The equation **A**x + **B**y = **C** can be rearranged to $y = -\dfrac{A}{B}x + \dfrac{C}{B}$. What can we conclude from this?

Example 1:   Solve 6x + 3y = 16 for y.

Solution: 6x + 3y = 16   subtract 6x from both sides
            3y = –6x + 16   divide both sides by 3
            $y = -2x + \dfrac{16}{3}$

            our KEY indicators

Remember: y = mx + b
           where **"m"** (the coefficient of x) is the **slope** of the equation and **"b"** is the **y-intercept**. For the equation 6x + 3y = 16, the slope is –2 and the y-intercept is $\dfrac{16}{3}$.

With these two KEY pieces of information, we can graph, or draw, the line.

6x + 3y = 16

Given various information about a linear equation, determine the "zeros", slope and y-intercept of the following.

1. $3x - 6y = 12$

      zeros: _____
      slope: _____
      y-intercept: _____

2. $x = 4y - 6$

      zeros: _____
      slope: _____
      y-intercept: _____

3. $y = 4x$

      zeros: _____
      slope: _____
      y-intercept: _____

4. $y + 2x = 8$

      zeros: _____
      slope: _____
      y-intercept: _____

5. $-2x - 3y = 5$

      zeros: _____
      slope: _____
      y-intercept: _____

6. $x + y = 0$

      zeros: _____
      slope: _____
      y-intercept: _____

7. $\dfrac{x}{2} + y = 9$

      zeros: _____
      slope: _____
      y-intercept: _____

8. $x + \dfrac{y}{3} = 4$

      zeros: _____
      slope: _____
      y-intercept: _____

9. $-2x + 3y = 6$

      zeros: _____
      slope: _____
      y-intercept: _____

10. $3x - y = 10$

      zeros: _____
      slope: _____
      y-intercept: _____

11. $x = 4y$

      zeros: _____
      slope: _____
      y-intercept: _____

12. $4x + y = 5$

      zeros: _____
      slope: _____
      y-intercept: _____

LESSON 27 – Equation of a Line Satisfying Certain Parameters

Write an equation, in standard form, satisfying the given conditions.

Example 1:   Passes through the point (2, –3) and parallel to the equation $3x - 4y = 5$.

Solution: Given a point and parallel to an equation, means we need to find the slope of the line, $m = \dfrac{\Delta y}{\Delta x}$, and then use the point-slope formula $y - y_1 = m(x - x_1)$.

$$3x - 4y = 5$$
$$-4y = -3x + 5$$
$$y = \tfrac{3}{4}x - \tfrac{5}{4}$$

$$m = \tfrac{3}{4}$$

Substitute $m = \tfrac{3}{4}$ and the point (2, –3) into the point-slope formula.

$$y - (-3) = \tfrac{3}{4}(x - 2)$$
$$y + 3 = \tfrac{3}{4}(x - 2)$$
$$4y + 12 = 3(x - 2)$$
$$4y + 12 = 3x - 6$$
$$18 = 3x - 4y$$

in standard form: $\boxed{3x - 4y = 18}$

Example 2:   Passes through the point (–1, 4) and perpendicular to $2x + 3y = 8$.

Solution: First find the slope of the equation.

$$2x + 3y = 8$$
$$3y = -2x + 8$$
$$y = -\tfrac{2}{3}x + \tfrac{8}{3}$$

Remember for perpendicular lines, that: $m_1 \cdot m_2 = -1$.

$$-\tfrac{2}{3} \cdot m_2 = -1$$
$$-\tfrac{3}{2} \cdot -\tfrac{2}{3} \cdot m_2 = -1 \cdot -\tfrac{3}{2}$$
$$m_2 = \tfrac{3}{2}$$

30

Given $m = \frac{3}{2}$ and the point $(-1, 4)$, substitute into the point-slope formula.

$$y - y_1 = m(x - x_1)$$
$$y - 4 = \tfrac{3}{2}(x - (-1))$$
$$y - 4 = \tfrac{3}{2}(x + 1)$$
$$2y - 8 = 3(x + 1) \quad \text{multiply by 2}$$
$$2y - 8 = 3x + 3 \quad \text{distribute the 3}$$
$$-11 = 3x - 2y$$

in standard form: $\boxed{3x - 2y = -11}$

Example 3: Perpendicular to $x - 2y = 7$ with y-intercept $(0, -3)$.

Solution: First find the slope of the equation.

$$x - 2y = 7$$
$$-2y = -x + 7$$
$$y = \tfrac{1}{2}x - \tfrac{7}{2}$$

Remember for perpendicular lines, that: $m_1 \cdot m_2 = -1$.

$$\tfrac{1}{2} \cdot m_2 = -1$$
$$\tfrac{2}{1} \cdot \tfrac{1}{2}m_2 = -1 \cdot \tfrac{2}{1}$$
$$m_2 = -2$$

Given $m = -2$ and the point $(0, -3)$, substitute into the point-slope formula.

$$y - y_1 = m(x - x_1)$$
$$y - (-3) = -2(x - 0)$$
$$y + 3 = -x \quad \text{distribute the } -2$$
$$3 = -x - y$$

in standard form: $\boxed{2x + y = -3}$

Find the equation of a line given various parameters. Put answer in standard form Ax + By = C.

1.   the y-intercept is 6 and the slope is 2

2.   two points on the line are (3, 2) and (–4, 6)

3.   going through the point (1, 4) with a slope of $\frac{3}{2}$

4.   parallel to the y-axis and going through the point (–3, –8)

5.   the linear equation goes through the points (–2, –1) and (6, 4)

6.   the line is perpendicular to 3x – 2y = 10 through the point (2, –2)

7.   a horizontal line through the point (4, –5)

8.   through the origin with a slope of 3

9.   the y-intercept is –2 and the slope is $-\frac{3}{4}$

10.   through the point (4, –5) and (–2, 3)

LESSON 28 – Graphing Linear Inequalities in Two Variables

This is just like graphing linear equalities except you need to shade in certain areas of the grid.

Example 1:   Graph the inequality $x + 2y \geq 6$.

Solution: Temporary substitute the inequality sign ($\geq$) with an equal sign ($=$) and solve for y.

$$x + 2y = 6$$
$$2y = -x + 6$$
$$y = -\tfrac{1}{2}x + 3$$

Graph the equality. If the inequality is $\leq$ or $\geq$, keep a solid line. If the inequality is $<$ or $>$, use a dashed line.

To decide which side of the line to shade, select the origin, (0, 0), and substitute in the **original inequality**.

$$0 + 2(0) \overset{?}{\geq} 6$$
$$0 + 0 \overset{?}{\geq} 6$$
$$0 \ngeq 6$$

Therefore, (0, 0) is not part of the graph and you need to shade the other half-plane.

It is a simple procedure:

Step 1: Graph as an equality.
Step 2: Solid or dashed line.
Step 3: Use (0,0) to find out if (0, 0) is in the shaded region
Step 4: Shade the appropriate half-plane.

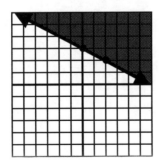

Example 2:   y < –3x + 1

Solution: y < –3x + 1 as an equality is in the slope-intercept form, y = mx + b.
               Therefore, m = –3 (slope) and b = 1 (y-intercept).

Step 1: Graph as an equality.
Step 2: Dashed line (<).
Step 3: (0, 0) is in the shaded region.
Step 4: Shade the appropriate region.
Step 5: Check by selecting any point in the shaded region.

m = –3 b = 1 (y-intercept) plot "b" on the y-axis slope = $\frac{\Delta y}{\Delta x}$ = $\frac{-3}{1}$ down 3, right 1 dashed line substitute (0, 0) y < –3x + 1 0 < 0 + 1 0 < 1	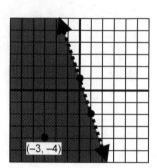	Check: Select any point in the shaded region. (–3, –4) Substitute into original inequality. y = < –3x + 1 –4 < –3(–3) + 1 –4 < 9 + 1 –4 < 10

Graph the following inequalities.

1.   y < x + 3

2.   y ≥ 3 – 3x

3.   y ≥ 4

4.   x + y > 2

5.   x – y ≥ 4

6.   y – 2x ≤ –3

7.   3(y – 2x) < 4

8.   3y – 5 > 2x – 7

9.   6x + 4y ≤ –x – 8

LESSON 30 – Exponent Rules and Distributive Property

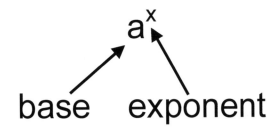

base   exponent

A. ⬚ Product Rule ⬚   When the bases are the same, add the exponents.

$$a^x \cdot a^y = a^{x+y}$$

Example 1: $4^3 \cdot 4^2 = 4^{3+2} = 4^5$

B. ⬚ Power Rule ⬚   Multiply the exponents.

$$(a^x)^y = a^{x \cdot y} = a^{xy}$$

Example 2: $(4^2)^3 = 4^{2 \cdot 3} = 4^6$ Example 3: $(c^2)^4 = c^{2 \cdot 4} = c^8$

C. ⬚ Quotient Rule ⬚   When the bases are the same, subtract the exponents.

$$\frac{a^x}{a^y} = a^{x-y}$$

Example 3: $\frac{m^5}{m^2} = m^{5-2} = m^3$

D. ⬚ Zero Rule ⬚   Anything, other than zero, to the zero power is 1.

Example 5: $x^0 = 1$ Example 7: $-4^0 = -1$ $(-1 \cdot 4^0 = -1 \cdot 1 = -1)$

Example 6: $5^0 = 1$ Example 8: $(-4)^0 = 1$

E. $\boxed{\text{Negative Exponent Rule}}$ $\qquad a^{-x} = \dfrac{1}{a^x}$

Example 9: $4^{-2} = \dfrac{1}{4^2} = \dfrac{1}{16}$ $\bigg|$ Example 12: $4x^{-3} = \dfrac{4}{x^3}$

Example 10: $(x^2)^{-2} = \dfrac{1}{(x^2)^2} = \dfrac{1}{x^{2\cdot 2}} = \dfrac{1}{x^4}$ $\bigg|$ Example 13: $2xy(5x^{-2}y + 6a^{-2}x^2y) =$

$\qquad$ or $\qquad (x^2)^{-2} = x^{2\cdot -2} = x^{-4} = \dfrac{1}{x^4}$ $\qquad\qquad \dfrac{10xy^2}{x^2} + \dfrac{12x^3y^2}{a^2}$

$\qquad\qquad\qquad\qquad\qquad\qquad\qquad\qquad \dfrac{10y^2}{x} + \dfrac{12x^3y^2}{a^2}$

Example 11: $8^{-3} = \dfrac{1}{8^3} = \dfrac{1}{512}$

Evaluate $x^{-1}y^2$ when $x = 2$ and $y = 3$.

$\quad$ Solution: $\quad x^{-1}y^2 = \dfrac{y^2}{x} = \dfrac{3^2}{2} = \dfrac{9}{2}$ or $x^{-1}y^2 = 2^{-1} \cdot 3^2 = \dfrac{1}{2} \cdot 9 = \dfrac{9}{2}$

Rewrite $\dfrac{x^2 x^3 y^{-2} z^4}{x^{-2} y^3 z}$ with all positive exponents.

$\quad$ Solution: $\quad \dfrac{x^2 x^3 y^{-2} z^4}{x^{-2} y^3 z} = \dfrac{x^2 x^3 x^2 z^4}{y^3 y^2 z} = \dfrac{x^{2+3+2} z^4}{y^{3+2} z} = \dfrac{x^7 z^4}{y^5 z} = \dfrac{x^7 z^{4-1}}{y^5} = \dfrac{x^7 z^3}{y^5}$

Rewrite $\dfrac{x^2 x^{-4} y^2 z^{-3}}{x^3 y^{-3} z^5}$ with all variables in the numerator.

$\quad$ Solution: $\quad \dfrac{x^2 x^{-4} y^2 z^{-3}}{x^3 y^{-3} z^5}$

$\qquad\qquad (x^2 x^{-4} x^{-3}) \cdot (y^2 y^3) \cdot (z^{-3} z^{-5}) =$
$\qquad\qquad (x^{2-4-3}) \cdot (y^{2+3}) \cdot (z^{-3-5}) =$
$\qquad\qquad x^{-5} y^5 z^{-8}$

Distributive Property distributes multiplication over addition. Some examples are

$$a(b + c) = a \cdot b + a \cdot c = ab + ac$$
$$6(3 + x) = 6 \cdot 3 + 6 \cdot x = 18 + 6x$$
$$-3(x + 4y) = -3 \cdot x + (-3) \cdot 4y = -3x + (-12y) = -3x - 12y$$
$$5x(x + 3) = 5x \cdot x + 5x \cdot 3 = 5x^2 + 15x$$
$$7(a + 2b + c) = 7 \cdot a + 7 \cdot 2b + 7 \cdot c = 7a + 14b + 7c$$

Use the exponent rules and distributive property to simplify the following.

1. $3x(4x^2 - 5x + 6)$

2. $-x^2(x^3 - 4x^2 - 3x + 7)$

3. $2x[3x^2 + 6(2x + 3)]$

4. $-a(a^2 - ab - 5b^2)$

5. $ab(c^2 - 3c + 4)$

6. $8\left(\dfrac{9x^2}{2} - \dfrac{3x}{4} + \dfrac{1}{8}\right)$

7. $24\left(\dfrac{x^2}{3} + \dfrac{x}{8} - \dfrac{5}{6}\right)$

8. $10y\left(10y^2 - 6y - \dfrac{3}{2y}\right)$

9. $-8e(4e^3 - 2e^2 + e + 3)$

10. $9f(-f^2 + 4f - \tfrac{1}{3})$

11. $5x^3z^4(3x^5 + 2x^2z^2 - 4xz^3)$

12. $(2a^2 - 3ac - c^3)(-5a^2c^2)$

13. $(-4y^5)^2$

14. $(5a^2b^3)(4ab^2)(-5a^3b^4)$

15. $\left(\dfrac{a^2b^2}{2}\right)(4ab + 8a^3b - 6b^5)$

LESSON 31 – Addition and Subtraction of Polynomials

There are two methods for this operation. Either perform the operation horizontally or vertically. Let me show you both ways.

HORIZONTALLY

Example 1: $(4a^2 + 3a - 6) + (3a + 8 - 2a^2)$

Solution: $4a^2 + 3a - 6 + 3a + 8 - 2a^2 =$ Remove grouping symbols.
$4a^2 - 2a^2 + 3a + 3a - 6 + 8 =$ Group like terms.
$(4a^2 - 2a^2) + (3a + 3a) + (-6 + 8)$ Combine like terms.
$2a^2 + 6a + 2$

Example 2: $3(x2 - 3x - 4) + (x - 5) - 2(x2 + 5x)$

Solution: $3x^2 - 9x - 12 + x - 5 - 2x^2 - 10x =$ Use Distributive Property.
$3x^2 - 2x^2 - 9x + x - 10x - 12 - 5 =$ Group like terms.
$(3x^2 - 2x^2) + (-9x + x - 10x) + (-12 - 5) =$ Combine like terms.
$x^2 - 18x - 17$

VERTICALLY – only after you use the Distributive Property.

Example 3: $(3x^3 + 16x^2 - 5x - 10) + (x^3 - 9x^2 + 6x - 4)$

Solution:

$$
\begin{array}{rrrr}
3x^3 & + \ 16x^2 & - \ 5x & - \ 10 \\
+ \ x^3 & - \ 9x^2 & + \ 6x & - \ 4 \\
\hline
4x^3 & + \ 7x^2 & + \ x & - \ 14 \\
\end{array}
$$

Example 4: $(16x^3 - 14x^2 - 7x + 8) + (-8x^3 - 2x^2 + 9x - 6)$

Solution:

$$
\begin{array}{rrrr}
16x^3 & - \ 14x^2 & - \ 7x & + \ 8 \\
+ \ -8x^3 & - \ 2x^2 & + \ 9x & - \ 6 \\
\hline
8x^3 & - \ 16x^2 & + \ 2x & + \ 2 \\
\end{array}
$$

Example 5: $(4a^3 - 4a^2 + 6a - 7) - (2a^3 - 6a^2 + 5a + 7)$

Solution: Remember in subtraction the signs in the subtrahend are changed.

$$\begin{array}{rrrrr}
 & 4a^3 & - \quad 4a^2 & + \quad 6a & - \quad 7 \\
+ & -2a^3 & + \quad 6a^2 & - \quad 5a & - \quad 7 \\
\hline
 & 2a^3 & + \quad 2a^2 & + \quad a & - \quad 14
\end{array}$$

Example 6: $(3x^2 + 4x - 11) + (2x^2 - 4x + 10) - (3x^2 - 5x + 6)$

Solution:

Vertically:

$$\begin{array}{rrrr}
 & 3x^2 & + \quad 4x & - \quad 11 \\
+ & 2x^2 & - \quad 4x & + \quad 10 \\
\hline
 & 5x^2 & + \quad 0 & - \quad 1 \\
+ & -3x^2 & + \quad 5x & - \quad 6 \\
\hline
 & 2x^2 & + \quad 5x & - \quad 7
\end{array}$$

To start, add the first two trinomials.

Then subtract the third trinomial.

Horizontally:

$3x^2 + 4x - 11 + 2x^2 - 4x + 10 =$ Remove grouping symbols from first
$3x^2 + 2x^2 + 4x - 4x - 11 + 10 =$ two trinomials, group and combine
$5x^2 - 1$ like terms.

$5x^2 - 1 - 3x^2 + 5x - 6 =$ Now subtract the third trinomial,
$5x^2 - 3x^2 + 5x - 1 - 6 =$ remembering to change the signs.
$2x^2 + 5x - 7$ Group and combine like terms.

or, remove the grouping symbols from all three trinomials, group and combine like terms:

$3x^2 + 4x - 11 + 2x^2 - 4x + 10 - 3x^2 + 5x - 6 =$
$(3x^2 + 2x^2 - 3x^2) + (4x - 4x + 5x) + (-11 + 10 - 6) =$
$2x^2 + 5x + (-7) =$
$2x^2 + 5x - 7$

PRACTICE MAKES PERFECT!

Simplify the following.

1. $(6x^2 - 5x - 8) - (4x^2 + 7x - 2)$

2. $3(3n^2 - 6n + 4) + 2(-n^2 + 7n - 8)$

3. $(4a^3 - 6a^2 + 8a - 1) - (2a^2 - 6a + 9)$

4. $(2y^3 + 5y^2 - 9y - 13) + (7y^2 - 8y^3 + 14)$

5. $2(5x^2 - 6x + 4) - 3(2x^2 + 5x - 3)$

6. $(4a^2 + 3a - 6) + (3a + 8 - 2a^2)$

7. $3(x^2 - 3x - 4) + (x - 5) - 2(x^2 + 5x)$

8. $(3x^3 + 16x^2 - 5x - 10) + (x^3 - 9x^2 + 6x - 4)$

9. $(16x^3 - 14x^2 - 7x + 8) + (-8x^3 - 2x^2 + 9x - 6)$

10. $(4a^3 - 4a^2 + 6a - 7) - (2a^3 - 6a^2 + 5a + 7)$

11. $(3x^2 + 4x - 11) + (2x^2 - 4x + 10) - (3x^2 - 5x + 6)$

12. $(2n^2 - 3m^2) - (n^2 + 6m^2 - mn)$

13. $(3x^2 - 6x - 2) - (-x^2 - 5x + 9)$

14. $(a^2 - 5a - 7) - (-a^2 - 8a + 7)$

15. $(3x^2 - 6x - 4) - (3x) - (9x - 3x^2 + 4)$

16. $(x^3 - x^2 + x) + (-5x^3 + 2x^2 - 4x + 1)$

17. $(2x + y) + (4x - 5y) - (7x + y)$

18. $(a^2b - 3ab^2 - ab^3) + (5ab^2 - 6a^2b^2)$

19. $(6n^2 - 4) - (3n + 2) - (n^2 + n) + (n - 5)$

20. $2(xy^2 - 3xy^2 + 3) + 4(2xy^2 - y^3 + xy^2)$

LESSON 32 – Multiplication of Binomials – FOIL

First Outer Inner Last

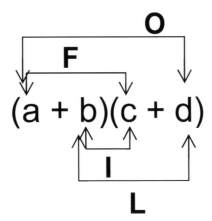

$(a + b)(c + d)$

First terms: $a \cdot c = ac$
Outer terms: $a \cdot d = ad$
Inner terms: $b \cdot c = bc$
Last terms: $b \cdot d = bd$

$(a + b)(c + d) = ac + ad + bc + bd$

Example 1: $(2a + 3b)(c - 4d)$

Solution: First terms: $2a \cdot c = 2ac$
Outer terms: $2a \cdot (-4d) = -8ad$
Inner terms: $3b \cdot c = 3bc$
Last terms: $3b \cdot (-4d) = -12bd$

$(2a + 3b)(c - 4d) =$
$2ac - 8ad + 3bc - 12bd$

Example 2: $(-4x + 3y)(x - 5y)$

Solution: First terms: $(-4x) \cdot x = -4x^2$
Outer terms: $(-4x) \cdot (-5y) = 20xy$
Inner terms: $3y \cdot x = 3xy$
Last terms: $3y \cdot (-5y) = -15y^2$

$(-4x + 3y)(x - 5y) =$
$-4x^2 + \textbf{20xy + 3xy} - 15y^2 =$

combine like terms
$-4x^2 + 23xy - 15y^2$

41

Example 3: $(6x - 5y)(-2x + 3y)$

Solution: First terms: $6x \cdot (-2x) = -12x^2$
Outer terms: $6x \cdot 3y = 18xy$
Inner terms: $(-5y) \cdot (-2x) = 10xy$
Last terms: $(-5y) \cdot 3y = -15y^2$

$(6x - 5y)(-2x + 3y) =$
$-12x^2 + \mathbf{18xy + 10xy} - 15y^2 =$
$-12x^2 + 28xy - 15y^2$

Example 4: $(4x + 3)^2$

Solution: $(4x + 3)^2 = (4x + 3)(4x + 3)$

F: $4x \cdot 4x = 16x^2$
O: $4x \cdot 3 = 12x$
I: $3 \cdot 4x = 12x$
L: $3 \cdot 3 = 9$

$(4x + 3)^2 =$
$16x^2 + 12x + 12x + 9 =$
$16x^2 + 24x + 9$

Example 5: $(2x - 5)(6x + 1)$

Solution: F: $2x \cdot 6x = 12x^2$
O: $2x \cdot 1 = 2x$
I: $-5 \cdot 6x = -30x$
L: $-5 \cdot 1 = -5$

$(2x - 5)(6x + 1)$
$12x^2 + 2x - 30x - 5 =$
$12x^2 - 28x - 5$

Example 6: $(a - 2b)(-3a + 5b)$

Solution: F: $a \cdot (-3a) = -3a^2$
O: $a \cdot 5b = 5ab$
I: $(-2b) \cdot (-3a) = 6ab$
L: $(-2b) \cdot 5b = -10b2$

$(a - 2b)(-3a + 5b) =$
$-3a^2 + 5ab + 6ab - 10b^2 =$
$-3a^2 + 11ab - 10b^2$

Multiply these binomials and simplify your answer whenever possible.

1. $(5x + 3)(2x - 5)$

2. $(a + 3b)(-2a - b)$

3. $(4a + 5c)^2$

4. $(-c + 3d)(2c + 3d)$

5. $(6x - 5y)(7x + y)$

6. $(c - 2d)(3c + d)$

7. $(5r + 2s)(3s + 2r)$

8. $(e + f)(e - f)$

9. $(6 + 5x)(-4x + 3)$

10. $(3x - 7y)^2$

11. $(2x^2 - 5)(3x^2 + 7)$

12. $(xy^2 + z)(xy^2 - z)$

13. $(-3a + 1)(5a + 6)$

14. $(2b^3 + 3)^2$

15. $(2a + 3)(4a - 7)$

16. $(4b - 9)(b + 3)$

17. $(7x - 2y)(3x + y)$

18. $(15a - 1)(4a + 3)$

19. $(5x + 3y)(6x - 5y)$

20. $(4y + 5z)(3y - 2z)$

VERTICAL

Example 1: $(3x^2 + 4x - 5)(2x - 3)$

Solution: Multiply by –3 first.

$$
\begin{array}{rrrr}
3x^2 & + \quad 4x & - & 5 \\
 & 2x & - & 3 \\
\hline
- \quad 9x^2 & - \quad 12x & + & 15 \\
6x^3 \quad + \quad 8x^2 & - \quad 10x & & \\
\hline
6x^3 \quad - \quad x^2 & - \quad 22x & + & 15
\end{array}
$$

Example 2: $(6a^2 - 3a + 2)(-a + 3)$

Solution:

$$
\begin{array}{rrrr}
6a^2 & - \quad 3a & + & 2 \\
 & - \quad a & + & 3 \\
\hline
18a^2 & - \quad 9a & + & 6 \\
-6a^3 \quad + \quad 3a^2 & - \quad 2a & & \\
\hline
-6a^3 \quad + \quad 21a^2 & - \quad 11a & + & 6
\end{array}
$$

HORIZONTAL

Example 3: $(3x^2 + 4x - 5)(2x - 3)$

Solution:

Rearrange: $(2x - 3)(3x^2 + 4x - 5)$
Use the Distributive Property: $2x(3x^2 + 4x - 5) = 6x^3 + 8x^2 - 10x$ **line 1**
Use the Distributive Property: $-3(3x^2 + 4x - 5) = -9x^2 - 12x + 15$ **line 2**

Add line 1 and line 2:

horizontal:

$(6x^3 + 8x^2 - 10x) + (-9x^2 - 12x + 15) =$
$6x^3 + (8x^2 - 9x^2) + (-10x - 12x) + 15 =$
$6x^3 + (-x^2) + (-22x) + 15$

$(3x^2 + 4x - 5)(2x - 3) = 6x^3 - x^2 - 22x + 15$

or, vertical: be sure to line up the variables correctly

$$
\begin{array}{rrrr}
6x^3 \quad + \quad 8x^2 & - & 10x & \\
- \quad 9x^2 & - & 12x & + \quad 15 \\
\hline
6x^3 \quad - \quad x^2 & - & 22x & + \quad 15
\end{array}
$$

Example 4: $(-a + 3)(6a^2 - 3a + 2)$

   Solution:

   Use Distributive Property: $(-a)(6a^2 - 3a + 2) = -6a^3 + 3a^2 - 2a$ **line 1**
   Use Distributive Property: $3(6a^2 - 3a + 2) = 18a^2 - 9a + 6$ **line 2**

   Add line 1 and line 2: $-6a^3 + (3a^2 + 18a^2) + (-2a - 9a) + 6$

   $(-a + 3)(6a^2 - 3a + 2) = -6a^3 + 21a^2 - 11a + 6$

Multiply these polynomials. (Remember to arrange exponents in descending order.)

1. $(y + 3)(y^2 - 5y + 4)$

2. $(2a - 3)(a^3 - 4a + 1)$

3. $(x^2 + 3x - 5)(x + 7)$

4. $(x - 6)(x^2 - 3x - 9)$

5. $(3b - 5)(2b^2 - 8b + 3)$

6. $(4x^2 - 5x + 3)(x - 6)$

7. $(c^2 - 2c + 4)(2c - 5)$

8. $(3a + 4)(12 - 3a + 2a^2)$

9. $(3y - 7)(4y^2 + y - 6)$

10. $(z^2 + 3z - 4)(4z - 5)$

11. $(3a + 4)(6a - 5)$

12. $(2b - 3)(3b^2 + b - 1)$

13. $(x + 3)(6x^2 + 11x - 10)$

14. $(2a + 1)(a^2 - 3a + 2)$

15. $(3a - 4)(3a - 4)(3a - 4)$

16. $(d^2 + 5d + 2)(3d - 1)$

17. $2(3a - a^2)(a + 2)$

18. $(y^2 + 1)(1 - 2y + 3y^2)$

19. $(x^2 - 3x + 1)(x^2 + 2x - 3)$

20. $(a - 2b)^2(a + 3b)^2$

LESSON 34 – Division of a Polynomial by a Monomial Divisor

To divide, break up the polynomial into separate terms, each term being divided by the divisor. Then divide each term. Check out these examples:

Example 1:

$$\frac{15x^3 + 12x^2 + 6x - 21}{3} =$$

$$\frac{15x^3}{3} + \frac{12x^2}{3} + \frac{6x}{3} - \frac{21}{3} =$$

$$5x^3 + 4x^2 + 2x - 7$$

Example 2:

$$\frac{16x^4 + 24x^3 - 8x^2 + 12x - 20}{4} =$$

$$\frac{16x^4}{4} + \frac{24x^3}{4} - \frac{8x^2}{4} + \frac{12x}{4} - \frac{20}{4} =$$

$$4x^4 + 6x^3 - 2x^2 + 3x - 5$$

Example 3:

$$\frac{16x^3 + 14x^2 - 8x - 6}{2} =$$

$$\frac{16x^3}{2} + \frac{14x^2}{2} - \frac{8x}{2} - \frac{6}{2} =$$

$$8x^3 + 7x^2 - 4x - 3$$

Example 4:

$$\frac{24x^3 + 17x^2 - 12x + 30}{3} =$$

$$\frac{24x^3}{3} + \frac{17x^2}{3} - \frac{12x}{3} + \frac{30}{3} =$$

$$8x^3 + \frac{17x^2}{3} - 4x + 10$$

Example 5:

$$\frac{4x^3 - 16x^2 + 11x - 8}{2x} =$$

$$\frac{4x^3}{2x} - \frac{16x^2}{2x} + \frac{11x}{2x} - \frac{8}{2x} =$$

$$2x^2 - 8x + \frac{11}{2} - \frac{4}{x}$$

> **NOTE**
>
> **If the divisor does not divide evenly, keep the fractional answer.**

Divide these polynomials by a monomial divisor.

1. $(36x^4 - 27x^3 + 81x^2 - 9x) \div (3x)$

2. $(16x^3 - 12x^2 - 24x + 40) \div (4)$

3. $(28x^3 - 42x^2 + 70x + 56) \div (7x)$

4. $(12a^3b^3c^3 - 20a^2b^2c^2 + 8abc) \div (4abc)$

5. $(48x^3 - 16x^2 + 20x - 32) \div (8x)$

46

6. $(30a^4 + 25a^3 - 40a^2 + 15a - 20) \div (5a)$

7. $(27a^3 + 18a^2 - 15a + 30) \div (3)$

8. $(8b^4 - 6b^3 + 12b^2 - 4b + 10) \div (2b)$

9. $(4a^4 + 8a^3b - 12a^2b^2) \div (4a^2)$

10. $(c^2d^2 + c - d) \div (cd)$

11. $(24cd^3 - 18c^2d - 12c) \div (-6c)$

12. $(-7y^3 - 21y^2 + 14y) \div (7y)$

13. $(6a - 12a^2 - 18a^3 + 36a^4) \div (6a)$

14. $(25x^4y^3 - 15x^2y^4 + 40xy^5) \div (-5xy)$

15. $(27x^3y^2 - 9x^2y + 18xy - 45x^2y^2) \div (9xy)$

16. $(10a^4 - 8a^3 + 16a^2 + 24a - 28) \div (-2a)$

17. $(40x^3 + 56x^2y - 64xy^2 + 24y^3) \div (8xy)$

18. $(-24x^3y^2z^2 + 32x^4y^3z^4) \div (4xy^2z)$

19. $(x^3 + 4x - 2x^2 - 8) \div (x)$

20. $(6x^3 - 8x^2 + 10x + 4) \div (-2x)$

LESSON 35 – Division of a Polynomial by a Binomial Divisor

We will now use a binomial (2 terms) as our divisor. It sets up a little different. Remember those two-digit divisors in elementary school. I'll show you the similarities.

Elementary school example: $4296 \div 24$

Solution:

```
            1 7 9
   24 | 4 2 9 6
      - 2 4
        1 8 9
      - 1 6 8
          2 1 6
        - 2 1 6
              0
```

Check:

```
    ×  1 7 9
          2 4
       7 1 6
     3 5 8
     4 2 9 6
```

Example 1: $(3x^3 - x^2 + x - 1) \div (x + 1)$

Solution: $(3x^3 - x^2 + x - 1) \div (x + 1) = 3x^2 - 4x + 5$

Step 1: $\dfrac{3x^3}{x} = 3x^2$. Place $3x^2$ above the x^2 term.

Step 2: Multiply $3x^2$ times $(x + 1)$. $3x^2(x + 1) = 3x^2 + 3x^2$.

Step 3: Subtract. Remember when subtracting, the signs change.

Step 4: $\dfrac{-4x^2}{x} = -4x$. Place $-4x$ above the x term.

Step 5: Multiply: $-4x(x + 1) = -4x^2 - 4x$

Step 6: Subtract.

Step 7: $\dfrac{5x}{x} = 5$. Place above the constant (5).

Step 8: Multiply: $5(x + 1) = 5x + 5$

Step 9: Subtract.

Step 10: Check your answer.

```
                Step    Step    Step
                 1       4       7
                3x²  -   4x  +   5
  x + 1 |  3x³  -   x²  +   x  +  5
        -  3x³  -  3x²               Step 3
             -  4x²  +   x
             +  4x²  +  4x          Step 6
                  +  5x  +   5
                  -  5x  -   5      Step 9
                            0       remainder
```

```
Step 10:
              3x²  -  4x  +  5
   ×                    x  +  1
              3x²  -  4x  +  5
   3x³  -  4x²  +  5x
   3x³  -   x²  +   x  +  5

Checked!
```

48

Example 2: $(3x^3 - x^2 - 6x - 12) \div (x - 2)$

Solution: $(3x^3 - x^2 - 6x - 12) \div (x - 2) = 3x^2 + 5x + 4 + \dfrac{-4}{x - 2}$

Step 1: $\dfrac{3x^3}{x} = 3x^2$. Place $3x^2$ above the x^2 term.

Step 2: Multiply: $3x^2(x - 2) = 3x^3 - 6x^2$.

Step 3: Subtract. Remember when subtracting, the signs change.

Step 4: $\dfrac{5x^2}{x} = 5x$. Place $5x$ above the x term.

Step 5: Multiply: $5x(x - 2) = 5x^2 - 10x$.

Step 6: Subtract.

Step 7: $\dfrac{4x}{x} = 4$. Place above the constant (12).

Step 8: Multiply: $4(x - 2) = 4x - 8$

Step 9: Subtract. In this problem, there is a remainder.

Step 10: Check your answer.

		Step 1		Step 4		Step 7	
		$3x^2$	$+$	$5x$	$+$	4	
$x - 2$	$3x^3$	$-$	x^2	$-$	$6x$	$-$	12
	$-\ 3x^3$	$+$	$6x^2$				(Step 3)
		$+$	$5x^2$	$-$	$6x$		
		$-$	$5x^2$	$+$	$10x$		(Step 6)
			$+$	$4x$	$-$	12	
			$-$	$4x$	$+$	8	(Step 9)
				$-$	4		remainder

Step 10:

$$
\begin{array}{r}
3x^2 + 5x + 4 \\
\times \qquad\quad x - 2 \\
\hline
-6x^2 - 10x - 8 \\
3x^3 + 5x^2 + 4x \\
\hline
3x^3 - x^2 - 6x - 8 \\
- 4 \\
\hline
3x^3 - x^2 - 6x - 12
\end{array}
$$

Checked!

Make certain the remainder is a fraction using the divisor as the denominator.

Divide these polynomials by a binomial divisor.

1. $(x^3 - 3x^2 + 3x - 1) \div (x + 2)$ 2. $(x^3 + 6x^2 + 12x + 8) \div (x + 2)$

3. $(x^3 + 5x^2 - 7x + 3) \div (x - 2)$ 4. $(x^3 + 6x^2 + 12x + 8) \div (x - 3)$

5. $(2x^2 - 7x - 8) \div (2x + 1)$ 6. $(x^3 - 1) \div (x + 1)$

7. $(9x^3 + 5x + 2) \div (3x + 2)$ 8. $(4x^4 - 5x^2 + 7) \div (2x - 3)$

9. $(8x^3 - 12x^2 + 6x - 1) \div (2x - 1)$ 10. $(8x^3 - 12x^2 + 6x - 1) \div (2x + 1)$

LESSON 37 – Common Monomial Factor (CMF)

Factoring, in algebra, requires an ability to recognize special situations along with knowing prime numbers. Prime numbers, by definition, have itself and one (1) as its only two factors. Single digit prime numbers are 2, 3, 5, and 7. With these concepts, let us begin to understand factoring.

We will begin with the common monomial factor (CMF). Look for this first and foremost when factoring.

Let us examine the five pairs of factors for 48. They are: (1)(48), (2)(24), (3)(16), (4)(12), and (6)(8). How can factoring fundamentals help in math? It helps when trying to "factor" a binomial (2 terms), a trinomial (3 terms), and a polynomial (more than 3 terms).

Let us begin by factoring a binomial. That is two terms. Examples of a term: x, 3x, $4x^2$.

Example: 2x + 6b

    Solution:

        2 is a factor of itself and also 6. $\dfrac{2x}{2} + \dfrac{6b}{2} = x + 3b$

        When we take a 2 out of 2x + 6b, we end up with 2(x + 3b).

This mathematics process of factoring is the removal of a common monomial (one term) factor. From the above example, I essentially took out a 2 from 2x, leaving an x, and took out a 2 from 6b, leaving 3b. The final result: 2x + 6b = 2(x + 3b).

More binomial factoring problems to practice:

    a. $16x^2 + 64y^2$
    b. $4a^3b^2c^4 - 18a^2b^3c^3$
    c. $9x^2 - 25y^2$
    d. $8 + 24a^2$
    e. $12x^4y^2 - 32a^2x^4$

Several trinomials with common monomial factor:

    f. $2x^2 + 6x + 10$
    g. $3a^2x + 6ax - 12x$

Let's examine each situation.

a.   What common factor is present in $16x^2 + 64y^2$? Certainly not the x^2 nor y^2. Okay, let's look at 16 and 64. This is where factoring knowledge comes in handy.

Factors of 16 are: 1 and **16**, 2 and 8, 4 and 4
Factors of 64 are: 1 and 64, 2 and 32, 4 and **16**, 8 and 8

The largest common factor of both 16 and 64 is 16. Therefore, 16 is the common monomial factor (CMF). Removing the 16 from both terms, **_and_** placing it outside the parenthesis, our answer is $16(x^2 + 4y^2)$.

b.   What common factor is present in $4a^3b^2c^4 - 18a^2b^3c^3$? At least a 2, a, b, and c. How many a's, b's, and c's? Pick a minimum of each term. For a, that would be a^2; for b, it would be b^2; and for c, it's c^3. Therefore, the CMF would be $2a^2b^2c^3$.

Removing the CMF from the original problem, what remains? In the first term it is 2ac and in the second terms, 9b.

The final answer is $2a^2b^2c^3(2ac - 9b)$.

c.   There is no CMF in $9x^2 - 25y^2$. However, this binomial is an example of a perfect square term minus another perfect square term. One needs to take the square root of each term, 3x and 5y, and have opposite signs for each factor. The final answer is $(3x + 5y)(3x - 5y)$. More about square minus square, cube plus cube, and cube minus cube in Lesson 38.

d. $8 + 24a^2$ has a CMF in each term. The magic CMF is 8. When 8 is removed from both terms, we end up with 1 and 3a2. Yes, we need a 1 to replace the 8. So the correct answer is 8(1 + 3a2).

e. $12x^4y^2 - 32a^2x^4$ has a CMF of $4x^4$. Removing the $4x^4$ from both terms leaves $3y^2 - 8a^2$. The final answer is $4x^4(3y^2 - 8a^2)$.

f.   In $2x^2 + 6x + 10$, 2 is the CMF in all three terms. Completely factored, $2(x^2 + 3x + 5)$ is the final answer.

g.   Factoring a 3x from the original problem, $3a^2x + 6ax - 12x$, we get $3x(a^2 + 2a - 6)$ which is fully factored.

Factoring a binomial, trinomial or polynomial by first removing a common monomial factor (CMF).

1. $10x^2 + 5x$

2. $15a^3 + 10a^2b^2 - 5a^2b$

3. $60t^4 - 4at^2 + 12t$

4. $30x^2y^2 + 45x^2y - 75x^2y^3$

5. $9x^4 - 18x^3 + 12x^2 - 30x$

6. $120h^5 + 100h^4 + 50h^3 + 10h$

7. $6x^5y - 15x^4y^2 + 20x^3y^3 + 6xy^5$

8. $7a^6 + 21a^5b^2 + 21a^2b^5 + 7a^4b^3$

9. $63x^6y^5z^4 - 105x^5y^4z^3 + 21x^4y^3$

10. $84x^8y^5 + 105x^3y^2 - 63x^2y^3$

11. $21r^2s^3t^4 + 30r^3s^2t^2 + 6r^2s^4t^5 + 18r^4s^2t^4$

12. $14x^3y^3z^4 - 28x^2y^3z^2 + 35x^5y^2z^3 - 49x^2y^4z^5$

13. $15a^3bc^2 + 25a^2b^2c^2 - 30a^4b^3c^4 + 60a^3b^2c^4$

14. $18L^2m^3n^4 - 36L^3m^3n^3 + 24L^4m^4n^5 + 48L^3m^2n^3$

15. $8x^3 - 16x^2 + 44x - 24$

16. $21a^2b^2 + 33ab^3 - 63a^3b + 15ab$

17. $20m^3n^3 - 28m^2n + 16mn^2$

18. $12x^2y^2 - 16x^3y + 20xy^2 - 32x^4y^3$

19. $121z^4 + 33z^2 - 66z^3 - 99z^5$

20. $2c^6 + 8c^5 - 42c^4$

LESSON 38 – Factoring a Binomial
It could be either a square minus a square,
a cube plus a cube, or a cube minus a cube.

First, one needs to know perfect square numerals. Here's some help. 1, 4, 9, 16, 25, 36, 49, 64, 81, and 100 are the first ten numbers squared. These squares are numbers to know. Then the cubes. 1, 8, 27, 64, 125, 216, 343, 512, 729, and 1000 are the first ten cubes. Wow! When you have memorized the above facts, we can proceed. Get that calculator working.

Here are some practice problems with answers:

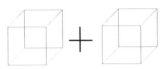

Example 1: $27x^3 + 64y^6$ cube plus cube

> Solution:
>
> There is a formula for cubes. Here's the scoop:
>
> $$a^3 + b^3 = (a + b)(a^2 - ab + b^2)$$
> $$a^3 - b^3 = (a - b)(a^2 + ab + b^2)$$
>
> So let's try to factor $27x^3 + 64y^6$. The cube root of $27x^3$ is $3x$ and the cube root of $64y^6$ is $4y^2$. So the first factor of the answer is $(3x + 4y^2)$. Now let's figure out the second factor. Using the factor $(3x + 4y^2)$, square the first term $(3x)$, which is $9x^2$. Then, multiply the two terms together, $(3x)(4y^2)$, which is $12xy^2$. Finally, square the second term $(4y^2)$ for $16y^4$. So, putting this altogether, the final answer is $(3x + 4y^2)(9x^2 - 12xy^2 + 16y^4)$.

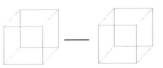

Example 2: $8a^3 - 125b^3$ cube minus cube

> Solution:
>
> Take the cube root of $8a^3$ and $125b^3$, getting $2a$ and $5b$, respectively. The first factor is $(2a - 5b)$. Use this factor to arrive at the second factor: square the first term, multiply the two terms together, and square the second term: $(2a)^2 + (2a)(5b) + (5b)^2 = 4a^2 + 10ab + 25b^2$. Putting the two factors together to get $(2a - 5b)(4a^2 + 10ab + 5b^2)$, which is the correct answer.

Example 3: $100x^4 - 25y^2$ square minus square $\boxed{} - \boxed{}$

Solution:

In Lesson 37, practice problem c, it was a square minus square factor problem. Again we have a square minus square problem. We must first check for a CMF and, low and behold, there is one. The CMF is 25. Removing the CMF, we arrive at $25(4x^4 - y^2)$. The second factor $(4x^4 - y^2)$ is a square minus square and needs to be factored further. We need to take the square root of each term, resulting in $(2x^2 + y)(2x^2 - y)$. The final answer is $25(2x^2 + y)(2x^2 - y)$.

Remember the formulas!

$a^2 - b^2 = (a + b)(a - b)$
$a^3 + b^3 = (a + b)(a^2 - ab + b^2)$ $\Big\}$ Remember these!
$a^3 - b^3 = (a - b)(a^2 + ab + b^2)$

Also, L⊙ ⊙ K for a common monomial factor every time you factor.

So far for factoring:

1.   Common monomial factor (CMF)
2.   If a binomial (2 terms):
        square minus square
        cube plus cube
        cube minus square

Factor the following completely.

1. $125c^3 + 64d^3$ 2. $1 - 169x^4$

3. $64x^6 - 1$ 4. $3x^3 - 75x$

5. $-144 + 25t^6$ 6. $9a^2 - \frac{1}{9}$

7. $(x + 3)^2 - x^2$ 8. $125a^3 + 512$

9. $27a^3 - 363ab^2$ 10. $(a + 1)^2 - (a - 1)^2$

11. $27x^3 - 363xy^2$ 12. $(x^2 - 4)^2 - 16$

LESSON 39 – Factoring Four Terms by Grouping

In the previous two lessons, we looked for a common monomial factor (CMF) in a group of terms and we examined binomials (two terms. Binomials are basically (i) square minus square, (ii) cube plus cube, and (iii) cube minus cube.

Now we will look at polynomials (many terms). The first group of polynomials is four terms. When we see four terms, we should think "grouping".

So to summarize to this point, we follow these guidelines:

1.   CMF – common monomial factor
2.   2 terms – binomials (square minus square, cube plus cube, cube minus cube)
3.   4 terms – grouping

Here is an example for factoring by grouping and how it is factored.

Example 1: $8a^2 - 10ab + 12ab - 15b^2$

Solution:

Step 1:   Group the first two terms and the last two terms.

$$(8a^2 - 10ab) + (12ab - 15b^2)$$

Step 2:   Find a CMF in $8a^2 - 10ab$. The CMF is 2a. Now remove, by dividing, the 2a from both terms, which leaves: $2a(4a - 5b)$. With this idea in mind, find a CMF in $12ab - 15b^2$. It is 3b. When dividing 3b into $12ab - 15b^2$, the answer is $4a - 5b$. So factored, it is $3b(4a - 5b)$.

Let's review what we have so far:

$8a^2 - 10ab + 12ab - 15b^2 =$
$(8a^2 - 10ab) + (12ab - 15b^2) =$
$2a(4a - 5b) + 3b(4a - 5b)$.

Now there is a CMF in both factored terms. It is $4a - 5b$. Extract $4a - 5b$ from both terms. What remains is $2a + 3b$.

Completely factored, $8a^2 - 10ab + 12ab - 15b^2 = (4a - 5b)(2a + 3b)$.

Using the FOIL method, let's check our work.

First   Outer   Inner   Last

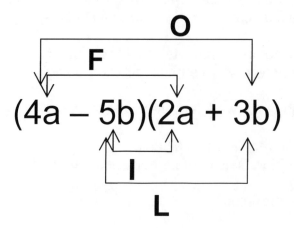

First terms: $4a \cdot 2a = 8a^2$
Outer terms: $4a \cdot 3b = 12ab$
Inner terms: $-5b \cdot 2a = -10ab$
Last terms: $-5b \cdot 3b = -15b^2$

$$8a^2 + 12ab - 10ab - 15b^2$$

Example 2: $2x^2 - 10x + 3xy - 15y$

Solution:

Step 1:   Group first two terms and last two terms.

$$(2x^2 - 10x) + (3xy - 15y)$$

Step 2:   Find a CMF in both groups. $2x^2 - 10x$ have $2x$ in common and $3xy - 15y$ have $3y$ in common.

Step 3: $\dfrac{2x^2 - 10x}{2x} = x - 5$ ($2x^2 - 10x$) factored is $2x(x - 5)$

$\dfrac{3xy - 15y}{3y} = x - 5$ ($3xy - 15y$) factored is $3y(x - 5)$

So far, we have

$$2x^2 - 10x + 3xy - 15y = 2x(x - 5) + 3y(x - 5)$$

Step 4:   Looking at $2x(x-5) + 3y(x-5)$, we have another CMF $(x-5)$. Removing it, we arrive at the two factors of $2x^2 - 10x + 3xy - 15y$.

$$2x(x-5) + 3y(x-5) = (x-5)(2x+3y)$$

Therefore, $2x^2 - 10x + 3xy - 15y = (x-5)(2x+3y)$

Step 5:   Check the answer by FOIL.

F: $x \cdot 2x = 2x^2$
O: $x \cdot 3y = 3xy$
I: $-5 \cdot 2x = -10x$
L: $-5 \cdot 3y = -15y$

$$2x^2 + 3xy - 10x - 15y$$
or
$$2x^2 - 10x + 3xy - 15y$$

Example 3: $3x^2y - 12x^2 + 9xy - 36x$

Solution:
Step 1:   Remove the CMF: $3x$

$$3x(xy - 4x + 3y - 12)$$

Step 2:   Group the first two terms and the last two terms.

$$3x[(xy - 4x) + (3y - 12)]$$

Step 3:   Remove "x" from the first two terms and "3" from the last two terms.

$$3x[x(y-4) + 3(y-4)]$$

Step 4:   Remove the CMF "$y-4$".

$$3x[(y-4)(x+3)]$$
$$3x(y-4)(x+3)$$

Step 5:   Check by FOIL.

Solution: $3x(y-4)(x+3)$

57

Factor the following by grouping.

1. $y^3 + 2y^2 - 3y - 6$

2. $9ab - 4 + 12a - 3b$

3. $x^3 + x^2 + 9x + 9$

4. $2c^2 + 20d - 8c - 5cd$

5. $2xy + 12 - 3y - 8x$

6. $12ab + 18a^2 - 3ac - 2bc$

7. $5x^2 + 15xy - 2xz - 6yz$

8. $xy^2 - 2y^2 - x + 2$

9. $10f^3 - 8f + 15f^2 - 12$

10. $y^3 + y^2 - 9y - 9$

11. $2ax - 2cx + ay - cy$

12. $a(b^2 - 4) + c(b^2 - 4)$

13. $-x - y + xy + 1$

14. $6a^2b - 72a + 18ab - 24a^2$

LESSON 40 – Review of Factoring
CMF, Binominals, and Grouping

Review factoring with these concepts in mind:

#1: Look for a CMF.

#2: If it's a binomial, check for square minus square, cube plus cube, or cube minus cube.

#3: Grouping with a four-term polynomial.

Now we'll practice to see if we can move forward.

Example 1: $x^2(y + 2) - 9(y + 2)$

Solution:

Find a CMF if present. The CMF is $(y + 2)$. Remove the CMF from both terms, arriving at $(y + 2)(x^2 - 9)$. ARE WE DONE?

NO! Why not? Correct, you can STILL factor the $(y^2 - 9)$. It is a square minus a square. $(x^2 - 9)$ factors into $(x + 3)$ and $(x - 3)$.

Result: $(y + 2)(x + 3)(x - 3)$

Example 2: $x^4 + x^3 + 8a^3x + 8a^3$

Solution:

Group the first two terms and the last two terms:

$$(x^4 + x^3) + (8a^3x + 8a^3)$$

LOOK for a CMF in both groups and remove it.

$(x^4 + x^3) = x^3(x + 1)$
$(8a^3x + 8a^3) = 8a^3(x + 1)$

We now have: $x^3(x + 1) + 8a^3(x + 1)$.

Again, look for a CMF in both groups and remove it, $(x + 1)$ is common to both. Now we have: $(x + 1)(x^3 + 8a^3)$. But $(x^3 + 8a^3)$ is a cube plus cube. It factors into $(x + 2a)(x^2 - 2ax + 4a^2)$.

Final answer: $(x + 1)(x + 2a)(x^2 - 2ax + 4a^2)$.

Now we are handling the factoring dilemmas.

Example 3: $x^4 - 16x^2$

Solution:
We have a CMF: x^2.

Removing x^2 from both terms we get: $x^2(x^2 - 16)$. Is this fully-factored? No. $(x^2 - 16)$ is a square minus a square. It factors into $(x + 4)$ and $(x - 4)$.

Final answer: $x^2(x + 4)(x - 4)$

Example 4: $x^3(x^2 - 9) - y^3(x^2 - 9)$

Solution:
Double trouble!!

First factor out the CMF of $(x^2 - 9)$. What remains is $(x^3 - y^3)$. Giving us $(x^2 - 9)(x^3 - y^3)$. Both of which need factoring again.

$(x^2 - 9)$ is a square minus square. $(x^3 - y^3)$ is a cube minus cube.

$$(x^2 - 9) = (x + 3)(x - 3)$$
$$(x^3 - y^3) = (x - y)(x^2 + xy + y^2)$$

Putting it altogether, we have: $(x + 3)(x - 3)(x - y)(x^2 + xy + y^2)$

Example 5: $16x^4 - 256y^4$

Solution:
Remove the CMF: $16(x^4 - 16y^4)$.

Factor $(x^4 - 16y^4)$, a square minus square: $(x^2 + 4y^2)(x^2 - 4y^2)$.

Factor $(x^2 - 4y^2)$, another square minus square: $(x + 2y)(x - 2y)$.

Finally we have our answer: $16(x^2 + 4y^2)(x + 2y)(x - 2y)$.

Factor the following or answer the question.

1. Factor: $(a - 1)^2 - (a + 1)^2$

2. Explain the error: $3k^3 - 12k^2 - 15k = (k - 5)(k + 3)$

3. Factor: $25x^4 - 225y^6$

4. Factor: $16c^3 - 4c^2d^2 - 4cd + d^3$

5. What is the common monomial factor for the expression $(8x^3 - 24x^2 + 18x)$?

6. Factor: $16 - (x - y)^2$

7. Factor: $x^3 - 9x$

8. True or false: $x^2 - 4x + 4 - y^2 = (x + y - 2)(x - y - 2)$

9. Factor completely: $36x^2 - 81y^2$

10. Given: $27 - 216e^3$

   a. What is the common monomial factor?
   b. Factor completely.

11. The middle term of the expanded binomial $(7s - 4t)^2$ is what?

12. Factor by grouping: $2ab - 7a + a^2 - 14b$

13. Factor: $4 + 3xy - 3y - 4x$

14. Factor: $5x^2y - 125y^3$

15. Given: $x^6 - 1$

   a. Factor as a difference of cubes.
   b. Factor as a difference of squares.

LESSON 41 – Factoring a Trinomial When the Coefficient of x^2 is 1
(Trial and Error)

Factoring a trinomial whose coefficient of the squared variable is +1, we can use the trial and error theory.

Example 1: $x^2 + 4x + 3$

Solution:

Step 1:	(x +)(x +)	set up this first
Step 2:	(x + 3)(x + 1)	only factors of 3 are (1)(3)
Step 3:	Check it using FOIL!	

$$F \rightarrow x^2$$
$$\boxed{\begin{array}{l} O \rightarrow x \\ I \rightarrow 3x \end{array}} = 4x$$
$$L \rightarrow 3$$

$x^2 + 4x + 3$ GOOD!

Example 2: $x^2 - 4x + 3$

Solution: Notice that this is the same as example 1 except for the signs.

Step 1:	(x −)(x −)
Step 2:	(x − 3)(x − 1)
Step 3:	Remember to check by using FOIL!

Now we have two locks!

#1: $x^2 + ax + b$, where both signs are positive,
must always be (x +)(x +).

#2: $x^2 - ax + b$, where first sign is negative and second sign is positive, must always be (x −)(x −).

However, if we have a two negative-sign trinomial or a positive-negative-sign trinomial, the signs of the factors will be one positive sign and one negative sign. The sign of the middle term will determine the largest factors' sign.

Factor the following.

1. $x^2 - 10x - 39$

2. $y^2 - 24y + 95$

3. $y^2 + 17y + 16$

4. $t^2 - 44t + 43$

5. $c^2 - 3x + 2$

6. $x^2 - 18x - 19$

7. $x^3 + 8x^2 + 15x$

8. $3a^2 - 33a + 54$

9. $a^2 + 26a + 133$

10. $r^2 + 15r + 26$

11. $a^2 + 29a - 62$

12. $h^2 - 6h + 9$

13. $x^3 - 18x^2 + 17x$

14. $-2x^2 - 4x + 70$

15. $x^2 - 15x - 16$

16. $w^2 + 51w + 144$

17. $a^2 - 16a + 28$

18. $b^2 + 11b + 18$

19. $k^2 - 10k + 25$

20. $-x^3 + 4x^2 - 3x$

LESSON 42 – Factoring a Trinomial When the Coefficient of x^2 is > 1

This is the final installment on understanding how to factor. It's factoring a trinomial whose x^2 coefficient is greater than 1. It involves grouping, setting up four terms to factor. In general, it looks like this: $Ax^2 + Bx + C$.

Let me explain a few things before your try. Remember, we are looking for two factors, when multiplied, to give us the required trinomial. So here it goes!

Example 1: $2x^2 – 7x – 15$

   Solution:

   The key here is to multiply the x^2 coefficient and the constant. In the above trinomial, that would be the 2 and –15. The result is –30.

   Next we examine what two factors of –30 has a sum or difference of –7. (That's the coefficient of the middle term.) Our choices are: (1)(–30), (2)(–15), (3)(–10), (5)(–6), (6)(–5), (10)(–3), (15)(–2), or (30)(–1). From these eight choices, there is one obvious answer: (3)(–10). Having selected these two factors, we rewrite the trinomial and make it a four-term polynomial: (a) $2x^2 + 3x – 10x – 15$ or (b) $2x^2 – 10x + 3x – 15$. Either way, our answer will be the same.

   Let us try (b) first. Group the first two terms and the last two terms:

   $2x^2 – 10x + 3x - 15$
   $(2x^2 – 10x) + (3x – 15)$.

   Next, take a common factor out of both groups: 2x in the first group and 3 in the second group.

   Removing the 2x from the two terms in the first group we have: $2x(x – 5)$. Likewise, the 3 is removed from the two terms in the second group, resulting in
   $3(x – 5)$.

   Combining everything we have done so far, we have:

   $2x^2 – 10x + 3x – 15$
   $(2x^2 – 10x) + (3x – 15)$
   $2x(x – 5) + 3(x – 5)$

   From the last step, we show a CMF (common monomial factor) in both groups. It is $(x – 5)$. Remove the $(x – 5)$ from both groups. What remains is $(2x + 3)$. The final answer is $(x – 5)(2x + 3)$.

Check your work by multiplying $(x - 5)$ times $(2x + 3)$.

F $(x)(2x) = 2x^2$
O $(x)(+3) = +3x$
I $(-5)(2x) = -10x$
L $(-5)(+3) = -15$

Combine O $(+3x)$ and I $(-10x)$ to get $-7x$.

Final check: $2x^2 - 7x - 15$.

When we try (a) $2x^2 + 3x - 10x - 15$, we should get the same answer.

Separate the $(2x^2 + 3x)$ from the $(-10x - 15)$.

$(2x^2 + 3x) - (10x - 15)$
$(2x^2 + 3x) - (10x + 15)$

> This negative sign changes the -15 to $+15$.

Find a CMF in both groups and remove it. In $(2x^2 + 3x)$, it is "x". In $(10x + 15)$, it is "5". This results in:

$x(2x + 3) - 5(2x + 3)$

Remove the CMF from both groups, which is $(2x + 3)$.

$(2x + 3)(x - 5)$

NOTE: your can reverse the factors also: $(x - 5)(2x + 3)$. Therefore, the answer can be $(x - 5)(2x + 3)$ or $(2x + 3)(x - 5)$.

Example 2: $6x^2 + x - 35$.

Solution:
    Product $(6 \cdot -35)$ is -210. Difference is 1.

Factors of -210 are: $(1)(-210)$, $(-1)(210)$, $(2)(-105)$, $(-2)(105)$, $(3)(-70)$, $(-3)(70)$, $(5)(-42)$, $(-5)(42)$, $(6)(-35)$, $(-6)(35)$, $(7)(-30)$, $(-7)(30)$, $(10)(-21)$, $(-10)(21)$, $(14)(-15)$, $(-14)(15)$. Our last try gets us a difference between factors of $+1$.

Rewrite the trinomial as a four-term polynomial.

$6x^2 - 14x + 15x - 35$

65

Group. (Note, put the negative as the second term and the positive as the third terms for grouping the four-term polynomial.)

$$(6x^2 - 14x) + (15x - 35)$$

Find the CMF for each and remove it.

$$2x(3x - 7) + 5(3x - 7)$$

Again, find the CMF and remove it.

$$(3x - 7)(2x + 5)$$

Check the final answer.

F: $(3x)(2x) = 6x^2$
O: $(3x)(5) = 15x$
I: $(-7)(2x) = -14x$
L: $(-7)(5) = -35$

Combining O ($15x$) and I ($-14x$) for the middle term of $+x$.

$$6x^2 + x - 35 \text{ voila!}$$

Example 3: $5x^2 - 31x - 28$.

Solution:
We know for sure that the factors need to look something like this $(5x \quad)(x \quad)$ because the only factors of 5 are itself and one.

Now examine -28. There are several factors besides itself and one. They are $(14)(2)$ and $(7)(4)$.

Taking the factors $(14)(2)$, we multiply 14 by 5 gives 70, that will be 70 ± 2 or 72 and 68. Whereas the factors $(7)(4)$ would be (7 times 5) $\pm$ 4, or 39 and 31. There is our 31.

Now substitute in 7 and 4 with their signs so $(5x + 7)(x - 4)$ gives $-13x$ for the middle term. Oops. Let's reverse the order: $(5x + 4)(x - 7)$ gives $-31x$ for the middle term. Therefore, $(5x + 4)(x - 7)$ is what we want. Check it using FOIL.

Factor the following.

1. $3x^2 + 8x + 4$

2. $3x^2 - 5x + 2$

3. $5x^2 - 7x - 12$

4. $5x^2 + 19x + 12$

5. $3x^2 - 5x - 2$

6. $6x^2 - 7x - 5$

7. $6x^2 + 19x + 10$

8. $16x^2 + 24x + 9$

9. $8x^2 - 27x + 9$

10. $6x^2 - 23x + 10$

11. $6x^2 - 5x - 6$

12. $21x^2 - 17x - 8$

13. $4x^2 + 7x + 3$

14. $28x^2 + 9x - 4$

15. $6x^2 + 16x + 10$

16. $9x^3 + 18x^2 + 9x$

17. $28x^2y + 2xy - 8y$

18. $12x^3 + 6x^2 - 18x$

19. $14x^2 - 8y^2 - 6xy$

20. $16x^2y^3 + 25x^4y + 40x^3y^2$

Lesson 43 – More Problems on Factoring Trinomials

Factor the following polynomials. There are **_NO_** primes.

1. $2a^6 + 8a^5 - 42a^4$

2. $15x^2 - 19x + 6$

3. $7 + 8a + a^2$

4. $12x^3 + 10x^2 - 12x$

5. $-2x^2 - 5x + 12$

6. $(x + 1)^2 + 3(x + 1) + 2$

7. $an^2 - 6an + 8a$

8. $x^2y^2 - 9x^2 - y^2 + 9$

9. $25y^4 - 100y^2$

10. $30x^3 + 51x^2 + 9x$

11. $12rs - 3s^2 - 12r^2$

12. $x(x^2 - 1) - 2(x^2 - 1)$

13. $45x^2 - 177xy - 12y^2$

14. $x^3 - x^2 - 4x + 4$

15. $a^3 + 2a^2 - 9a - 18$

16. $(x - 2)^2 - (y - 3)^2$

17. $(x + 3)^2 - 7(x + 3) + 10$

18. $-2x^2 - 24x + 170$

19. $2x^4 - 162$

20. $3x^2 + 10x - 8$

LESSON 45 – Solving Quadratic Equations by Factoring

The general form of a quadratic equation is $Ax^2 + Bx + C = 0$, where "A", "B", and "C" are real numbers and $A \neq 0$.

We must first set the quadratic equation equal to zero (0). Factor (if possible), then set each factor equal to zero (0).

Example 1: $a^2 + 5a + 4 = 0$

    Solution:

        Step 1:   Try to factor.

$$a^2 + 5a + 4 = 0$$
$$(a + 4)(a + 1) = 0$$

        Step 2:   Set each factor equal to zero (0).
        Step 3:   Solve each equation.

$$a + 4 = 0 \qquad a + 1 = 0$$
$$a = -4 \qquad\quad a = -1$$

        Step 4:   Check both roots in the **original** equation.

$$
\begin{array}{ll}
a = -4 & a = -1 \\
a^2 + 5a + 4 = 0 & a^2 + 5a + 4 = 0 \\
(-4)2 + 5(-4) + 4 = 0 & (-1)2 + 5(-1) + 4 = 0 \\
16 - 20 + 4 = 0 & 1 - 5 + 4 = 0 \\
-4 + 4 = 0 & -4 + 4 = 0 \\
0 \overset{\checkmark}{=} 0 & 0 \overset{\checkmark}{=} 0
\end{array}
$$

    Solution: $\{-4, -1\}$

You'll notice that the answer (roots) are always put in braces { }. The order is immaterial. However, I prefer to list the smaller root first.

Example 2: $x^2 + 3x - 4 = 0$

    Solution:

        Step 1: $x^2 + 3x - 4 = 0$
                    $(x + 4)(x - 1) = 0$

        Steps 2 and 3: $x + 4 = 0 \qquad\qquad x - 1 = 0$
                            $x = -4 \qquad\qquad\quad x = 1$

Step 4: $x = -4$ $x = 1$

$x^2 + 3x - 4 = 0$ $x^2 + 3x - 4 = 0$
$(-4)^2 + 3(-4) - 4 = 0$ $(1)^2 + 3(1) - 4 = 0$
$16 - 12 - 4 = 0$ $1 + 3 - 4 = 0$
$4 - 4 = 0$ $4 - 4 = 0$
$0 \overset{\vee}{=} 0$ $0 \overset{\vee}{=} 0$

Solution: $\{-4, 1\}$

Example 3: $c^2 + 3c = 0$

Solution:
Step 1: $c^2 + 3c = 0$
$c(c + 3) = 0$

Steps 2 and 3: $c = 0$ $c + 3 = 0$
$c = -3$

Step 4: $c = 0$ $c = -3$

$c^2 + 3c = 0$ $c^2 + 3c = 0$
$(0)^2 + 3(0) = 0$ $(-3)^2 + 3(-3) = 0$
$0 + 0 = 0$ $9 - 9 = 0$
$0 \overset{\vee}{=} 0$ $0 \overset{\vee}{=} 0$

Solution: $\{-3, 0\}$

Example 4: $2a^2 - 3a - 2 = 0$

Solution:
Step 1: $2a^2 - 3a - 2 = 0$
$(2a + 1)(a - 2) = 0$

Steps 2 and 3: $2a + 1 = 0$ $a - 2 = 0$
$a = -\frac{1}{2}$ $a = 2$

Step 4: $a = -\frac{1}{2}$ $a = 2$

$$2a^2 - 3a - 2 = 0$$ $$2a^2 - 3a - 2 = 0$$
$$2(-\tfrac{1}{2})^2 - 3(-\tfrac{1}{2}) - 2 = 0$$ $$2(2)^2 - 3(2) - 2 = 0$$
$$2(\tfrac{1}{4}) + \tfrac{3}{2} - 2 = 0$$ $$2(4) - 6 - 2 = 0$$
$$\tfrac{2}{4} + \tfrac{3}{2} - 2 = 0$$ $$8 - 6 - 2 = 0$$
$$\tfrac{1}{2} + \tfrac{3}{2} - 2 = 0$$ $$0 \overset{\checkmark}{=} 0$$
$$\tfrac{4}{2} - 2 = 0$$
$$2 - 2 = 0$$
$$0 \overset{\checkmark}{=} 0$$

Solution: $\{-\frac{1}{2}, 2\}$

Example 5: $\dfrac{2}{b-1} = \dfrac{b}{b+2}$

Solution:

Cross-multiply: $2(b + 2) = b(b - 1)$
Expand: $2b + 4 = b^2 - b$
Set equal to 0: $0 = b^2 - 3b - 4$

Step 1: $0 = b^2 - 3b - 4$
            $0 = (b - 4)(b + 1)$

Steps 2 and 3: $b - 4 = 0$ $b + 1 = 0$
                   $b = 4$ $b = -1$

Step 4: $b = 4$ $b = -1$

$$\dfrac{2}{b-1} = \dfrac{b}{b+2}$$ $$\dfrac{2}{b-1} = \dfrac{b}{b+2}$$
$$\dfrac{2}{4-1} = \dfrac{4}{4+2}$$ $$\dfrac{2}{-1-1} = \dfrac{-1}{-1+2}$$
$$\dfrac{2}{3} = \dfrac{4}{6}$$ $$\dfrac{2}{-2} = \dfrac{-1}{1}$$
$$\dfrac{2}{3} \overset{\checkmark}{=} \dfrac{2}{3}$$ $$-1 \overset{\checkmark}{=} -1$$

Solution: { 1, 4}

71

Solve these quadratic equations by factoring.

1. $x^2 - 4x = 0$

2. $2x^2 - 4 = -7x$

3. $x^2 + 6x + 9 = 0$

4. $x^2 - 3x = 10$

5. $3x(2x + 3) = 0$

6. $(x - 2)(x + 3) = 6$

7. $6a^2 + 11a = 72$

8. $m^2 + 9 = 10m$

9. $4a^2 = 8a + 5$

10. $6b^2 = b + 1$

11. $f^2 = 24 - 5f$

12. $(x - 5)(x - 2) = 28$

13. $5a^2 + 13a - 6 = 0$

14. $12x^2 = 2x + 2$

15. $3x^2 = 3$

16. $4a^2 + 7 = 29a$

17. $3x^2 + 5x = 2$

18. $2x(x + 1) = 84$

19. $2a^2 - 32a = 0$

20. $x^2 + 15 = -8x$

LESSON 46 – Irrational Numbers

An **IRRATIONAL NUMBER**, by definition, is an number which cannot be expressed as an integer or the quotient of two integers. The word **SURD** is given to any number that is irrational. Some examples of surds are $\sqrt{5}$, $\sqrt{17}$, $\sqrt[3]{20}$, $\sqrt[4]{7}$, $\sqrt{39}$ and π. Radicals that can be found exactly are rational. Some examples of rational numbers are $\sqrt{9}$, $\sqrt{16}$, $\sqrt{25}$), and many others. This understanding is necessary in order to comprehend Completing the Square and the Quadratic Formula, which are the topics of the next two lessons.

Here are some examples in simplifying a radical:

Example 1: $\sqrt{32}$

    Solution: $32 = 2 \cdot 2 \cdot 2 \cdot 2 \cdot 2 = 4 \cdot 4 \cdot 2 = 16 \cdot 2$

$$\sqrt{32} = \sqrt{4 \cdot 4 \cdot 2} = \sqrt{4}\,\sqrt{4}\,\sqrt{2} = 2 \cdot 2 \cdot \sqrt{2} = 4\sqrt{2}$$

    or

$$\sqrt{32} = \sqrt{16 \cdot 2} = \sqrt{16}\,\sqrt{2} = 4\sqrt{2}$$

Example 2: $\sqrt{48}$

    Solution: $48 = 2 \cdot 2 \cdot 2 \cdot 2 \cdot 3 = 4 \cdot 4 \cdot 3 = 16 \cdot 3$

$$\sqrt{48} = \sqrt{4 \cdot 4 \cdot 3} = \sqrt{4}\,\sqrt{4}\,\sqrt{3} = 2 \cdot 2 \cdot \sqrt{3} = 4\sqrt{3}$$

    or

$$\sqrt{48} = \sqrt{16 \cdot 3} = \sqrt{16}\,\sqrt{3} = 4\sqrt{3}$$

Example 3: $\sqrt{72}$

    Solution: $72 = 2 \cdot 2 \cdot 2 \cdot 3 \cdot 3 = 4 \cdot 9 \cdot 2 = 36 \cdot 2$

$$\sqrt{72} = \sqrt{4 \cdot 9 \cdot 2} = \sqrt{4}\,\sqrt{9}\,\sqrt{2} = 2 \cdot 3 \cdot \sqrt{2} = 6\sqrt{2}$$

    or

$$\sqrt{72} = \sqrt{36 \cdot 2} = \sqrt{36}\,\sqrt{2} = 6\sqrt{2}$$

Example 4: $\sqrt{112}$

Solution: $112 = 2 \cdot 2 \cdot 2 \cdot 2 \cdot 7 = 4 \cdot 4 \cdot 7 = 16 \cdot 7$

$$\sqrt{112} = \sqrt{4 \cdot 4 \cdot 7} = \sqrt{4} \sqrt{4} \sqrt{7} = 2 \cdot 2 \cdot \sqrt{7} = 4\sqrt{7}$$

or

$$\sqrt{112} = \sqrt{16 \cdot 7} = \sqrt{16} \sqrt{7} = 4\sqrt{7}$$

Simplify the following expressions. Express answer in simplest radical form.

1.	$\sqrt{225}$	2.	$\sqrt{40}$	3.	$\sqrt{120}$
4.	$2\sqrt{32}$	5.	$5\sqrt{72}$	6.	$\sqrt{676}$
7.	$9\sqrt{90}$	8.	$\sqrt{324}$	9.	$12\sqrt{50}$
10.	$6\sqrt{45}$	11.	$10\sqrt{75}$	12.	$4\sqrt{108}$
13.	$\sqrt{128}$	14.	$\sqrt{864}$	15.	$\sqrt{7225}$
16.	$-2\sqrt{4}$	17.	$\sqrt{144}$	18.	$\sqrt{12}$
19.	$4\sqrt{125}$	20.	$-5\sqrt{48}$	21.	$-\sqrt{96}$
22.	$\sqrt{300}$	23.	$3\sqrt{75}$	24.	$6\sqrt{63}$
25.	$5\sqrt{200}$	26.	$3\sqrt{32}$	27.	$6\sqrt{150}$
28.	$-7\sqrt{400}$	29.	$5\sqrt{180}$	30.	$4\sqrt{98}$
31.	$16\sqrt{80}$	32.	$-3\sqrt{121}$	33.	$10\sqrt{72}$
34.	$8\sqrt{56}$	35.	$4\sqrt{45}$	36.	$6\sqrt{32}$
37.	$-2\sqrt{96}$	38.	$5\sqrt{125}$	39.	$12\sqrt{320}$
40.	$-3\sqrt{60}$	41.	$\sqrt{625}$	42.	$6\sqrt{242}$
43.	$-7\sqrt{28}$	44.	$9\sqrt{720}$	45.	$10\sqrt{500}$

LESSON 47 – Solving Quadratic Equations by Completing the Square

Lesson 45 showed how to solve a quadratic equation, $Ax^2 + Bx + C = 0$, where A, B, and C are real numbers and $A \neq 0$, by factoring. However, not every quadratic equation can be factored by using integers.

Consider this equation: $x^2 - 4x + 1 = 0$. Since it cannot factor easily, we will use a method know as **Completing the Square**.

The step for Completing the Square are:

Step 1: Collect all variables on the left side of the equation and all constants on the right side of the equation.

Step 2: Divide B by 2. Square the result and add to both sides of the equation. Simplify the equation

Step 3: Since the left side of the equation is now a perfect square, we can factor it.

Step 4: Find the square root of both sides.

Step 5: Solve for "x".

Example 1: $x^2 - 4x + 1 = 0$

Solution: $B = -4$

Step 1: $x^2 - 4x = -1$

Step 2: $B = -4$

$$\frac{B}{2} = \frac{-4}{2} = -2$$

$$(-2)^2 = 4$$

$x^2 - 4x + 4 = -1 + 4$
$x^2 - 4x + 4 = 3$

Adding 4 to $x^2 - 4x$ is an example of Completing the Square. The trinomial $x^2 - 4x + 4$ is the square of $x - 2$.

Step 3: $(x - 2)^2 = 3$

Step 4: $\sqrt{(x - 2)^2} = \pm\sqrt{3}$
$x - 2 = \pm\sqrt{3}$

75

Step 5: $x - 2 = \pm\sqrt{3}$

$x = 2 \pm \sqrt{3}$

Solution: The original equation, $x^2 - 4x + 1 = 0$, has two solutions; $2 + \sqrt{3}$ and $2 - \sqrt{3}$.

Example 2: $x^2 - 6x + 2 = 0$

Solution: $B = -6$

Step 1: $x^2 - 6x = -2$

Step 2: $x^2 - 6x \mathbf{+ 9} = -2 \mathbf{+ 9}$

$x^2 - 6x + 9 = 7$

Step 3: $(x - 3)^2 = 7$

Step 4: $\sqrt{(x - 3)^2} = \pm\sqrt{7}$

$x - 3 = \pm\sqrt{7}$

Step 5: $x = 3 \pm \sqrt{7}$

Solution: $x = 3 + \sqrt{7}$ and $x = 3 - \sqrt{7}$

Check:
$(3 + \sqrt{7})^2 - 6(3 + \sqrt{7}) + 2 = 0$
$(3 + \sqrt{7})(3 + \sqrt{7}) - 18 - 6\sqrt{7} + 2 = 0$
$9 + 3\sqrt{7} + 3\sqrt{7} + 7 - 18 - 6\sqrt{7} + 2 = 0$
$9 + 6\sqrt{7} + 7 - 18 - 6\sqrt{7} + 2 = 0$
$(9 + 7 - 18 + 2) + (6\sqrt{7} - 6\sqrt{7}) = 0$
$16 - 18 + 2 + 0 = 0$
$-2 + 2 = 0$
$0 \overset{\checkmark}{=} 0$

$(3 - \sqrt{7})^2 - 6(3 - \sqrt{7}) + 2 = 0$
$(3 - \sqrt{7})(3 - \sqrt{7}) - 18 + 6\sqrt{7} + 2 = 0$
$9 - 3\sqrt{7} - 3\sqrt{7} + 7 - 18 + 6\sqrt{7} + 2 = 0$
$9 - 6\sqrt{7} + 7 - 18 - 6\sqrt{7} + 2 = 0$
$(9 + 7 - 18 + 2) + (-6\sqrt{7} + 6\sqrt{7}) = 0$
$16 - 18 + 2 + 0 = 0$
$-2 + 2 = 0$
$0 \overset{\checkmark}{=} 0$

Example 3: $x^2 - 8x = 2$

Solution: $B = -8$

Step 1: $x^2 - 8x = 2$

Step 2: $x^2 - 8x \mathbf{+ 16} = 2 \mathbf{+ 16}$

Step 3: $(x - 4)^2 = 18$

Step 4: $\sqrt{(x - 4)^2} = \pm\sqrt{18}$

$x - 4 = \pm\sqrt{18}$

$x - 4 = \pm3\sqrt{2}$

Step 5: $x = 4 \pm 3\sqrt{2}$

Solution: $4 + 3\sqrt{2}$ and $4 - \sqrt{2}$

Check:
$(4 + 3\sqrt{2})^2 - 8(4 + 3\sqrt{2}) = 2$
$(4 + 3\sqrt{2})(4 + 3\sqrt{2}) - 32 - 24\sqrt{2} = 2$
$16 + 12\sqrt{2} + 12\sqrt{2} + 18 - 32 - 24\sqrt{2} = 2$
$16 + 24\sqrt{2} + 18 - 32 - 24\sqrt{2} = 2$
$(16 + 18 - 32) + (24\sqrt{2} - 24\sqrt{2}) = 2$
$34 - 32 + 0 = 2$
$2 \overset{\checkmark}{=} 2$

$(4 - 3\sqrt{2})^2 - 8(4 - 3\sqrt{2}) = 2$
$(4 - 3\sqrt{2})(4 - 3\sqrt{2}) - 32 + 24\sqrt{2} = 2$
$16 - 12\sqrt{2} - 12\sqrt{2} + 18 - 32 + 24\sqrt{2} = 2$
$16 - 24\sqrt{2} + 18 - 32 + 24\sqrt{2} = 2$
$(16 + 18 - 32) + (-24\sqrt{2} + 24\sqrt{2}) = 2$
$34 - 32 + 0 = 2$
$2 \overset{\checkmark}{=} 2$

Solve the following quadratic equations by completing the square. Express any irrational roots in simplest form.

1. $x^2 - 2x = 20$

2. $z^2 - 6z - 321 = 6$

3. $a^2 + a = 5$

4. $x^2 + 12x - 2 = 0$

5. $t^2 - 4t - 3 = 0$

6. $d^2 + 14d + 5 = 0$

7. $x^2 + 8x = 10$

8. $c^2 + 16c = 132$

9. $2t^2 + 12t = 18$
   hint: divide all terms by 2

10. $a^2 + 6a - 1147 = 0$

11. $x^2 + 28x - 60 = 0$

12. $4a^2 + 12a + 5 = 0$

LESSON 48 – Solving Quadratic Equations Using the Quadratic Formula

The coefficients of the general formula, **$ax^2 + bx + c = 0$**, are used in the Quadratic Formula:

$$x = \frac{-b \pm \sqrt{b^2 - 4ac}}{2a}$$

where "a", "b", and "c" are obtained from the equation.

Steps for solving a quadratic equation:

Step 1: Simplify the equation and transpose all terms so that they are on the same side of the equation and equal to 0.

Step 2: Select the values of "a", "b" and "c" as shown in the Quadratic Formula

Step 3: Substitute the values for "a", "b" and "c" into the Quadratic Formula.

Step 4: Simplify the Quadratic Formula and solve for "x".

Step 5: Check the roots in the **original** quadratic equation.

Let us look closely at the first example as we proceed step-by-step.

Example 1: $x^2 + 3x - 40 = 0$

Solution:

Step 1: Already equal to 0.

Step 2: $a = 1$, $b = 3$, $c = -40$

Step 3: $x = \dfrac{-b \pm \sqrt{b^2 - 4ac}}{2a} = \dfrac{-3 \pm \sqrt{(3)^2 - 4(1)(-40)}}{2(1)}$

Step 4: $\dfrac{-3 \pm \sqrt{(3)^2 - 4(1)(-40)}}{2(1)} = \dfrac{-3 \pm \sqrt{9 + 160}}{2} =$

$\dfrac{-3 \pm \sqrt{169}}{2} = \dfrac{-3 \pm 13}{2}$

$x = \dfrac{-3 + 13}{2} = \dfrac{10}{2} = 5 \qquad\qquad x = \dfrac{-3 - 13}{2} = \dfrac{-16}{2} = -8$

Step 5:   x = 5   x = –8

$x^2 + 3x - 40 = 0$ $x^2 + 3x - 40 = 0$
$(5)^2 + 3(5) - 40 = 0$ $(-8)^2 + 3(-8) - 40 = 0$
$25 + 15 - 40 = 0$ $64 - 24 - 40 = 0$
$40 - 40 = 0$ $40 - 40 = 0$
$0 \overset{\checkmark}{=} 0$ $0 \overset{\checkmark}{=} 0$

Solution: {–8, 5}

Example 2: $x^2 + 4x = 21$

Solution:

Step 1: $x^2 + 4x - 21 = 0$

Step 2:   a = 1, b = 4, c = –21

Step 3: $x = \dfrac{-b \pm \sqrt{b^2 - 4ac}}{2a} = \dfrac{-4 \pm \sqrt{(4)^2 - 4(1)(-21)}}{2(1)}$

Step 4: $x = \dfrac{-4 \pm \sqrt{(4)^2 - 4(1)(-21)}}{2(1)} = \dfrac{-4 \pm \sqrt{16 + 84}}{2} =$

$\dfrac{-4 \pm \sqrt{100}}{2} = \dfrac{-4 \pm 10}{2}$

$x = \dfrac{-4 + 10}{2} = \dfrac{6}{2} = 3$ $x = \dfrac{-4 - 10}{2} = \dfrac{-14}{2} = -7$

Step 5:   x = 3   x = –7

$x^2 + 4x = 21$ $x^2 + 4x = 21$
$(3)^2 + 4(3) = 21$ $(-7)^2 + 4(-7) = 21$
$9 + 12 = 21$ $49 - 28 = 21$
$21 \overset{\checkmark}{=} 21$ $21 \overset{\checkmark}{=} 21$

Solution: {–7, 3}

Solve the following quadratic equations using the Quadratic Formula.

1. $a^2 + 4a = 6$

2. $x^2 + 0.9x + 0.1 = 0$

3. $\dfrac{y^2}{5} - \dfrac{5y}{4} = 1$

4. $\dfrac{1.5}{y - 3} = 2y$

5. $2 = 3x^2 + 2x$

6. $4x^2 + 8x - 3 = 0$

7. $\dfrac{a + 4}{2a} = \dfrac{a - 1}{a + 1}$

8. $3y = 2 - y^2$

9. $n + \dfrac{1}{n} = 3$

10. $-3x = -x^2 + 10$

11. $7s = 5 - 5s^2$

12. $x^2 + (x + 1)^2 = 841$

LESSON 49 – A Review of Quadratic Equations

Solve the following quadratic equation by any method.

1. $x^2 - 2 = \dfrac{7x}{2}$

2. $3x^2 + 4 - 13x = 0$

3. $0 = a^2 - a - 12$

4. $16x^2 + 34x - 15 = 0$

5. $n - \dfrac{1}{n} = 3$

6. $y^2 - 3y = 1$

7. $12x^2 - x - 35 = 0$

8. $a^2 - 10a = 10$

9. $x^2 - 7x + 6 = -4$

10. $(3x)(2x + 3) = 0$

11. $x - 30 = -42x^2$

12. $y^2 - 2y = 3$

13. $2a^2 + 6a + 1 = 0$

14. $(3x + 1)^2 - (2x - 1)^2 + 5 = 0$

LESSON 50 – Systems of Equations Solved by Elimination
by Either Addition or Subtraction

The procedure is as follows:

Step 1:   Simplify both equations by removing parentheses and/or clearing fractions, if need be.

Step 2:   Put the unknown quantities on the left side of the equal signs and the constants to the other side and then combine any like terms.

Step 3A: Select a variable to eliminate in both equations. If the constant of the variable is the same for both equations and the signs are opposite, add the two equations. If not, subtract.

Step 3B: If the two constants are unlike, multiply each equation by the other coefficient of the variable. Then proceed to add or subtract, depending upon the signs.

Step 4:   Once one of the two variables is eliminated, the result is a simple equation which you can solve.

Step 5:   Substitute that value in one of the **original** equations and solve.

Step 6:   The result should give you solutions for BOTH variables which need to be checked for correctness.

Let us review several examples.

Example 1: $\begin{cases} x + y = 10 & \text{(A)} \\ x - y = 4 & \text{(B)} \end{cases}$

Solution:

Step 1:   Since there are no parentheses or fractions, proceed to step 2.

Step 2:   In both equations, the variables are on one side and the constants on the other, so we go the step 3.

Step 3:   Select a variable to eliminate. If the coefficients are identical and have opposite signs, choose it. In the example, choose "y".

$$\begin{array}{ccccc} x & + & y & = & 10 \\ x & - & y & = & 4 \\ \hline 2x & + & 0 & = & 14 \end{array} \text{ Add both equations together.}$$

Step 4: Solve for "x".

$$2x = 14$$
$$x = 7$$

Step 5: Substitute the value of "x" in either **original** equation, and solve for "y".

$x + y = 10$	or	$x - y = 4$
$7 + y = 10$		$7 - y = 4$
$y = 3$		$y = 3$

Step 6: Check it!

Equation (A)	Equation (B)
$x + y = 10$	$x - y = 4$
$7 + 3 = 10$	$7 - 3 = 4$
$10 \overset{\checkmark}{=} 10$	$4 \overset{\checkmark}{=} 4$

Solution: $x = 7$ and $y = 3$

Example 2: $\begin{cases} 5x + y = 4 & \text{(A)} \\ 3x - 2y = -8 & \text{(B)} \end{cases}$

Solution:

Step 1: No parentheses or fractions. Proceed to step 2.

Step 2: Variables on the left, constants on the right. Proceed to step 3.

Step 3: Select a variable to eliminate, "y". Why "y"? The "y's" have opposite signs and you only need to multiply equation (A) by 2.

$$
\begin{array}{rcccccc}
2 \cdot (& 5x & + & y & = & 4 &) \\
& 3x & - & 2y & = & -8 &
\end{array}
\quad \rightarrow \quad
\begin{array}{rcccc}
10x & + & 2y & = & 8 \\
3x & - & 2y & = & -8 \\
\hline
13x & & & = & 0
\end{array}
$$

Step 4: Solve for "x".

$$13x = 0$$
$$x = 0$$

Step 5: Substitute x = 0 in either of the **original** equations.

Equation (A)   or   Equation (B)
  5x + y = 4   3x − 2y = −8
  5(0) + y = 4   3(0) − 2y = −8
  y = 4   −2y = −8
                                y = 4

Step 6: Check it!

Equation (A)   or   Equation (B)
  5(0) + 4 = 4   3(0) − 2(4) = −8
  0 + 4 = 4   0 − 8 = −8
  4 $\overset{\checkmark}{=}$ 4   −8 $\overset{\checkmark}{=}$ −8

Solution: x = 0 and y = 4

Example 3: $\begin{cases} m = 11 + n & \text{(A)} \\ 3m = 3 - 2n & \text{(B)} \end{cases}$

Solution:

Step 1: No parentheses or fractions. Proceed to step 2.

Step 2: Need to move the "n" in both equations to the left side. When doing this, remember that the sign of the variable changes when crossing the equal sign.

$$m - n = 11 \quad \text{(A)}$$
$$3m + 2n = 3 \quad \text{(B)}$$

Step 3: Select a variable, "n" to eliminate. See example 2 Step 3 as to why

$$2 \cdot (\; m - n = 11 \;) \;\rightarrow\; \begin{array}{rcrcr} 2m & - & 2n & = & 22 \\ 3m & + & 2n & = & 3 \\ \hline 5m & & & = & 25 \end{array}$$

Step 4: Solve for "m".

$$5m = 25$$
$$m = 5$$

84

Step 5:   Substitute m = 5 into either **original** equation.

	Equation (A)	or	Equation (B)

Equation (A)   or   Equation (B)
  m = 11 + n   3m = 3 – 2n
  5 = 11 + n   3(5) = 3 – 2n
  –6 = n   15 = 3 – 2n
                               12 = –2n
                               –6 = n

Step 6:   Check it!

Equation (A)   or   Equation (B)
  m = 11 + n   3m = 3 – 2n
  5 = 11 + (–6)   3(5) = 3 – 2(–6)
  5 $\overset{\checkmark}{=}$ 5   15 = 3 + 12
                               15 $\overset{\checkmark}{=}$ 15

Solution: m = 5 and n = –6

Example 4: $\begin{cases} \dfrac{3x + 8}{5} = \dfrac{3y - 1}{2} & \text{(A)} \\[2mm] \dfrac{x + y}{2} = 3 + \dfrac{x - y}{2} & \text{(B)} \end{cases}$

Solution:
Step 1:   ALERT!!! WE HAVE FRACTIONS!!

In equation (A), cross multiply.

$$(3x + 8)(2) = (5)(3y - 1)$$
$$6x + 16 = 15y - 5$$

In equation (B), remove the fractions by multiplying **_all_** three terms by 2.

$$2\left(\frac{x + y}{2}\right) = 2(3) + 2\left(\frac{x - y}{2}\right)$$
$$x + y = 6 + x - y$$

Step 2:   Variables to the left, constants to the right. Combine like terms.

$$6x - 15y = -21$$
$$2y = 6 \qquad \text{(the "x" canceled out)}$$

85

Step 3: Solve for "y".

$$2y = 6$$
$$y = 3$$

Step 4: Substitute y = 3 into the original equation (A).

$$\frac{3x + 8}{5} = \frac{3(3) - 1}{2}$$
$$\frac{3x + 8}{5} = \frac{9 - 1}{2}$$
$$\frac{3x + 8}{5} = \frac{8}{2}$$

Step 5: Solve for "x".

$$2(3x + 8) = 40 \qquad \text{cross multiply}$$
$$6x + 16 = 40$$
$$6x = 24$$
$$x = 4$$

Step 6: Check it!

Equation (A)

$$\frac{3x + 8}{5} = \frac{3y - 1}{2}$$
$$\frac{3(4) + 8}{5} = \frac{3(3) - 1}{2}$$
$$\frac{3(4) + 8}{5} = \frac{9 - 1}{2}$$
$$\frac{3(4) + 8}{5} = \frac{8}{2}$$
$$\frac{12 + 8}{5} = \frac{8}{2}$$
$$\frac{20}{5} = \frac{8}{2}$$
$$4 \overset{\checkmark}{=} 4$$

Equation (B)

$$\frac{x + y}{2} = 3 + \frac{x - y}{2}$$
$$\frac{4 + 3}{2} = 3 + \frac{4 - 3}{2}$$
$$\frac{7}{2} = 3 + \frac{1}{2}$$
$$\frac{7}{2} = 3\tfrac{1}{2}$$
$$3\tfrac{1}{2} \overset{\checkmark}{=} 3\tfrac{1}{2}$$

Solution: x = 4 and y = 3

Solve these systems of equations by either addition or subtraction.

1. $4a - 7b = 13$
   $2a - 7b = 3$

2. $3c - 2d = 13$
   $4c + 2d = 8$

3. $x + y = 0$
   $9x - 5y = 42$

4. $6x - 10y = 4$
   $x + y = 14$

5. $2x + 3y = 8$
   $3x + y = 5$

6. $2x - 3y = -8$
   $5x + 2y = -1$

7. $2x + 5y = 8$
   $3x - 2y = -7$

8. $5x + 2y = 61$
   $3x - 2y = 43$

9. $x - 4 = \dfrac{y}{2}$

   $0.5x + y = -3$

10. $x + y = 8$

    $\dfrac{x}{2} + \dfrac{2y}{3} = 4$

11. $6x + 3y = 48$
    $4x - y = 26$

12. $3x + 2y = 0$
    $x - 5y = 17$

13. $8x + 6y = 5$
    $2x + y = 1$

14. $-8x - 3y = 23$
    $2x - 5y = -23$

LESSON 51 – Systems of Equations Solved by Substitution

The procedure for solving by substitution is as follows:

Example 1: $\begin{cases} 6a + x = 12 & \text{(A)} \\ 2a + x = 8 & \text{(B)} \end{cases}$

Solution:

Step 1: Using one of the equations, solve for one of the unknown variables in terms of the other variable.

Equation (A)

$6a + x = 12$

$x = -6a + 12$

Equation (B)

$2a + x = 8$

$x = -2a + 8$

Step 2: Substitute this into the other equation.

Equation (B)

$2a + x = 8$

$2a + (-6a + 12) = 8$

Equation (A)

$6a + x = 12$

$6a + (-2a + 8) = 12$

Step 3: Solve for "a".

Equation (B)

$-4a + 12 = 8$

$-4a = -4$

$a = 1$

Equation (A)

$4a + 8 = 12$

$4a = 4$

$a = 1$

Step 4: Substitute the known value (a = 1) into the other equation.

Equation (A)

$6a + x = 12$

$6(1) + x = 12$

$6 + x = 12$

$x = 6$

Equation (B)

$2a + x = 8$

$2(1) + x = 8$

$2 + x = 8$

$x = 6$

Step 5. Check it!

Equation (A)

$6a + x = 12$

$6(1) + 6 = 12$

$6 + 6 = 12$

$12 \overset{\checkmark}{=} 12$

Equation (B)

$2a + x = 8$

$2(1) + 6 = 8$

$2 + 6 = 8$

$8 \overset{\checkmark}{=} 8$

Solution: a = 1 and x = 6

Example 2: $\begin{cases} 2a - 5b = 3 & \text{(A)} \\ 3b + a = 7 & \text{(B)} \end{cases}$

Solution:

Step 1: Solve for "a" in equation (B).

$$3b + a = 7$$
$$a = -3b + 7$$

Step 2: Substitute for "a" in equation (A).

$$2a - 5b = 3$$
$$2(-3b + 7) - 5b = 3$$

Step 3: Solve for "b".

$$-6b + 14 - 5b = 3$$
$$-11b + 14 = 3$$
$$-11b = -11$$
$$b = 1$$

Step 4: Substitute b = 1 into equation (B).

$$3b + a = 7$$
$$3(1) + a = 7$$
$$3 + a = 7$$
$$a = 4$$

Step 5: Check it!

Equation (A)   Equation (B)
$$2a - 5b = 3$$ $$3b + a = 7$$
$$2(4) - 5(1) = 3$$ $$3(1) + 4 = 7$$
$$8 - 5 = 3$$ $$3 + 4 = 7$$
$$3 \overset{\checkmark}{=} 3$$ $$7 \overset{\checkmark}{=} 7$$

Solution: a = 4 and b = 1

Example 3: $\begin{cases} 2x - 5y = -4 & \text{(A)} \\ x + y = 5 & \text{(B)} \end{cases}$

Solution:

Step 1: Solve for "y" in equation (B).

$$x + y = 5$$
$$y = -x + 5$$

Step 2: Substitute for y in equation (A).

$$2x - 5y = -4$$
$$2x - 5(-x + 5) = -4$$

Step 3: Solve for "x".

$$2x + 5x - 25 = -4$$
$$7x - 25 = -4$$
$$7x = 21$$
$$x = 3$$

Step 4: Substitute x = 3 into equation (B).

$$x + y = 5$$
$$3 + y = 5$$
$$y = 2$$

Step 5: Check your work!

Equation (A)	Equation (B)
$2x - 5y = -4$	$x + y = 5$
$2(3) - 5(2) = -4$	$3 + 2 = 5$
$6 - 10 = -4$	$5 \overset{\checkmark}{=} 5$
$-4 \overset{\checkmark}{=} -4$	

Solution: x = 3 and y = 2

Solve these systems of equations by substitute.

1. $m = 6n + 3$
   $m + 2n = 5$

2. $a - 5b = -13$
   $2a + b = 7$

3. $a = \frac{2}{3}b$
   $b + 6a = 30$

4. $4(x - 2y) = 8$
   $x + 6y = 2$

5. $y = 6x - 1$
   $3x - 3y = -2$

6. $a + 2b = 0$
   $\frac{5a}{6} - \frac{b}{3} = 6$

7. $3x - y = 1$
   $y = -3x + 2$

8. $y = x - 8$
   $x + 5y = 2$

9. $y = 3x$
   $x + y = 8$

10. $0.3(x - 1) = 2y$
    $7y = x$

11. $x = 2 - y$
    $y = x$

12. $6y - 3x = -8$
    $3x = 4 - 6y$

13. $x + 3y = 9$
    $x = 4y + 2$

14. $2x = 4y + 10$
    $5x - 2y = 17$

15. $y = 1 - x$
    $x = y - 3$

16. $x = 3y - 5$
    $x + 4y = 5$

LESSON 53 – A Review of Solving Systems of Equations

Solve these systems of equations by addition, subtraction, or substitution.

1. $y = a + 2$
    $2a + y = 11$

2. $e + f = 8$
    $e - 3f = 4$

3. $6x + 10y = 10$

    $9x = 4y + 53$

4. $\dfrac{x}{2} + \dfrac{y}{4} = 18$

    $\dfrac{x}{2} + \dfrac{y}{8} = 14$

5. $4p = 3q$
    $3p - q = 15$

6. $m - n = 4$
    $m - 6 = 2(n - 6)$

7. $4x + 2y = 20$
    $4x = 5y + 6$

8. $x - 5y = 2$
    $2x + y = 4$

9. $2.4 = 0.3a + 0.4b$
    $5a = 2 + 6b$

10. $3x - 5y = 8$
    $4x = 5y + 12$

11. $2x + 5y = 26$
    $-3x - 4y = -25$

12. $y = 2x + 1$
    $x + y = 1$

13. $t + u = 11$
    $(10t + u) - (10u + t) = 27$

14. $\dfrac{c}{2} + \dfrac{d}{3} = -4$
    $c + d = -10$

15. $3x + 2y = 4$
    $\frac{1}{3}(2x + y) = 1$

16. $r + s + t = 180$
    $r = s + t$
    $s = 4t$

    hint: replace r in the first equation by the second equation and then solve

92

LESSON 54 – Story Problems
Distance, Rate, Time

Example 1: A car4 travels 55 miles per hour (mph) for 10 hours. How far did it travel?

Solution: Distance = Rate • Time $\qquad$ D = R • T

$$D = \frac{55 \text{ miles}}{\text{hours}} \cdot \frac{10 \text{ hours}}{1} = 550 \text{ miles}$$

Example 2: A car travels 30 mph faster than a truck. Both vehicles leave from the same location and travel in opposite directions. After 5 hours and 500 miles between them, what is the rate of the car and the truck?

Solution:

	Rate	•	Time	=	Distance
Car	x	•	5	=	5x
Truck	x – 30	•	5	=	5(x – 30)

$$
\begin{aligned}
(\text{Distance of Car}) + (\text{Distance of Truck}) &= \text{Total Distance} \\
5x + 5(x - 30) &= 500 \\
5x + 5x - 150 &= 500 \\
10x - 150 &= 500 \\
10x &= 650 \\
x &= 65 \text{ mph}
\end{aligned}
$$

Rate of car: 65 mph
Rate of truck: 35 mph

Example 3: How long will it take a car, traveling at 55 mph, to pass a truck, which has a 3-hour head start and travels at 40 mph?

Solution:

	Rate	•	Time	=	Distance
Car	55	•	x	=	55x
Truck	40	•	x + 3	=	40(x + 3)

$$(\text{Distance of Car}) = (\text{Distance of Truck})$$

$$
\begin{aligned}
55x &= 40(x + 3) \\
55x &= 40x + 120 \\
15x &= 120 \\
x &= 8 \text{ hours}
\end{aligned}
$$

The car must travel 8 hours to pass the truck.

Example 4.   Two trains leave Union Station at 2:30 PM traveling in opposite directions. At 7 PM, how far apart are they if Train A's speed is 25 mph faster than Train B, which travels at 40 mph?

	Rate	•	Time	=	Distance
Train A	65	•	4.5	=	65(4.5)
Train B	40	•	4.5	=	40(4.5)

$$\begin{aligned} \text{Total Distance (D)} &= \text{(Distance of Train A) + (Distance of Train B)} \\ D &= 65(4.5) + 40(4.5) \\ D &= 282.5 + 180 \\ D &= 472.5 \text{ miles} \end{aligned}$$

Example 5:   A plane travels from Baltimore to Chicago in 2 hours. The return trip takes $1\frac{1}{2}$ hours. The distance between the two cities is 1200 miles. Find the speed of the plane and the speed of the wind.

Solution: $D = R \cdot T$

Let x = speed of the plane
Let y = speed of the wind

$$(x + y) \cdot 1\tfrac{1}{2} = 1200 \quad \text{(A)} \qquad \text{Chicago to Baltimore}$$
$$(x - y) \cdot 2 = 1200 \quad \text{(B)} \qquad \text{Baltimore to Chicago}$$

Divide equation (A) by $1\frac{1}{2}$ and equation (B) by 2.

$$x + y = 800$$
$$x - y = 600$$

Solve by elimination:

$$\begin{aligned} 2x &= 1400 \\ x &= 700 \qquad \text{speed of plane} \\ y &= 100 \qquad \text{speed of the wind} \end{aligned}$$

Solve these distance, rate, and time story problems.

1.   A cruise boat takes 45 minutes to travel downstream with a 5-mph current. The return trip against the current takes 1 hour and 10 minutes. Find (a) the rate of the cruise boat and (b) the distance traveled one way.

2.   A car averages 24 mph driving through a city and then 52 mph on the highway. The total distance traveled was 133 miles. How long did it take to drive through the city if the entire trip took 2 hours and 55 minutes?

3. A plane, flying with the wind, travels between two cities in 2 hours. Returning, against the wind, the plane travels only $\frac{2}{3}$ of the distance in 2 hours. Find the speed of the wind if the speed of the plane in calm air is 250 mph.

4. Michelle rode her bike from home to the repair shop and then walked home. She spent 10 minutes riding and 20 minutes walking. If Michelle's walking speed is 12 mph less then her biking speed, find the distance from her house to the repair shop.

5. At 2:30 P.M., a small plane had been flying one hour when a change of wind direction doubled its average ground speed. If the entire trip of 860 miles took $2\frac{1}{2}$ hours, (a) how far did the plane travel in the first hour and (b) in the last 30 minutes?

6. Anna leaves Avon at noon biking to Batavia at 16 mph. At 1 P.M., Bruce leaves Batavia towards Avon at 20 mph. If the distance between Avon and Batavia is 70 miles, at what time does Anna and Bruce meet?

7. Two planes leave O'Hare Airport in Chicago at the same time, one traveling east and the other west. The average speed of the eastbound plane is 60 mph more than the speed of the westbound plane. After $2\frac{1}{2}$ hrs of flying time, the planes are 4150 miles apart. (a) What are their speeds? (b) The eastbound plane traveled how many more miles then the westbound plane?

8. Ric jogs to baseball practice at 10 mph and gets a ride back home at 60 mph. The ride home took 15 minutes less than his jogging. How far did he jog and for how long?

9. It usually takes a bus 20 minutes to travel the 12 miles from City Hall to the airport down Broad Street. However, from 4 to 6 P.M., the bus will only travel 10 miles in the same length of time. If a bus leaves City Hall on the hour and every 15 minutes after that, and if it takes 20 minutes to get from a bus to an airplane, what is the last bus Harold can take from City Hall to get on a plane leaving at 5:50 P.M.?

10. A jogger travels 10 miles in an hour and 25 minutes. He averages 8 mph on level ground and 6 mph over hilly ground. What part of the 10 miles is on level ground?

11. A boat is traveling 30 mph slower than a car. If the car travels 126 miles in the same time as the boat travels 56 miles, find the rate of each.

12. At 1:30 P.M., Matt left Bel Air for White Marsh, cycling at 20 mph. At 2:00 P.M., Luke left White Marsh for Bel Air, cycling at 24 mph. If the distance from Bel Air to White Marsh is 32 miles, at what time did the boys meet?

LESSON 55 – Story Problems
Coins

Example 1: Fifty quarters and dimes have a total value of $11. How many quarters and dimes are there?

Solution:

Let q = number of quarters
Let d = number of dimes

0.25 = value of a quarter
0.10 = value of a dime

$$q + d = 50 \qquad \text{(A)}$$
$$0.25q + 0.10d = 11 \quad \text{(B)}$$

Multiply equation (B) by 100 to remove the decimals.

$$q + d = 50 \qquad \text{(A)}$$
$$25q + 10d = 1100 \quad \text{(B)}$$

Solve by elimination. Multiply equation (A) by –10.

$$-10q - 10d = -500$$
$$25q + 10d = 1100$$

Solve for "q".

$$15q = 600$$
$$q = 40$$

Substitute q = 40 in equation (A).

$$q + d = 50$$
$$40 + d = 50$$
$$d = 10$$

Check: $40(0.25) + 10(0.10) = 11$
             $10 + 1 = 11$
             $11 \overset{\checkmark}{=} 11$

Solution: 40 quarters and 10 dimes

Example 2:   Jake has some nickels and quarters. He has 33 coins altogether with $3.75 more in quarters than nickels. How many quarters and nickels does he have?

Solution:

$$n + q = 33 \qquad \text{(A)}$$
$$0.25q = \$3.75 + 0.05n \qquad \text{(B)}$$

Multiply equation (B) by 100 to remove the decimals.

$$n + q = 33 \qquad \text{(A)}$$
$$25q = 375 + 5n \qquad \text{(B)}$$

Solve by substitution. Solve equation (A) for "n".

$$n = 33 - q$$

Substitute in equation (B).

$$25q = 375 + 5n$$
$$25q = 375 + 5(33 - q)$$
$$25q = 375 + 165 - 5q$$
$$30q = 540$$
$$q = 18$$

Substitute q = 18 in equation (A).

$$n + q = 33$$
$$n + 18 = 33$$
$$n = 15$$

Check: $n + q = 33$ $0.25q = 3.75 + 0.05n$
          $15 + 18 = 33$ $0.25(18) = 3.75 + 0.05(15)$
          $33 \overset{\checkmark}{=} 33$ $4.5 = 3.75 + 0.75$
                               $4.5 \overset{\checkmark}{=} 4.5$

Solution: 18 quarters and 15 nickels

Solve these coin problems.

1. Fifty coins in quarters and dimes have a total value of $7.55. How many coins of each type are there?

2. Penny has 24 coins in nickels and dimes. Their value is $1.65. How many of each are there?

3. A collection has 25 coins, composed of nickels and quarters. If there are 3 more nickels than quarters, what is the total value of the coins?

4. Daphne counted her change and found she had $1.10 in pennies, nickels, and dimes. Of the 28 coins, there were 4 more pennies then nickels. Determine the number of each type of coin?

5. Mortimer has some nickels and quarters. There are 33 coins in all, with $3.75 more in quarters than in nickels. How many of each are there?

6. The total value of 42 nickels, dimes and quarters is $5.60. Determine the total number and value of each type of coin if we know the quantity of nickels and quarters is 32?

7. Your collection of quarters and half-dollars totals $7.50. There are three times as many quarters as half-dollars. How many of each are there?

8. The value of a bag filled with quarters and dimes is $27.80. If each quarter were replaced by a dime and each dime were replaced by a quarter, the value of the coins would be $31.70. How many of each type of coin is in the bag?

9. Barney has 50 coins in all, comprised of nickels and quarters. He had a dollar more in nickels than quarters. How many of each are there?

LESSON 56 – Story Problems
Digits

Example 1:   The sum of the digits of a two-digit number is 9. The number is 12 times the tens digit. What is the number?

Solution:

Let t = tens digit
Let u = ones digit
number = 10t + u

$$t + u = 9 \quad \text{(A)}$$
$$10t + u = 12t \quad \text{(B)}$$

Use substitution. Solve equation (A) for "u" and substitute into equation (B). Solve for "t"

$$t + u = 9$$
$$u = 9 - t$$

$$10t + u = 12t$$
$$10t + (9 - t) = 12t$$
$$9t + 9 = 12t$$
$$9 = 3t$$
$$3 = t$$

Substitute t = 3 into equation (A). Solve for "u".

$$t + u = 9$$
$$3 + u = 9$$
$$u = 6$$

Check the solution.

Equation (A)
$$t + u = 9$$
$$3 + 6 = 9$$
$$9 \overset{\checkmark}{=} 9$$

Equation (B)
$$10t + u = 12t$$
$$10(3) + 6 = 12(3)$$
$$30 + 6 = 36$$
$$36 \overset{\checkmark}{=} 36$$

Solution: The number is 36.

Example 2: The sum of the digits of a two-digit number is 15. The tens digit is one-half of three times the units digit. What is the number?

Solution:

Let t = tens digit
Let u = ones digit
number = 10t + u

$t + u = 15$ (A)

$t = \dfrac{3u}{2}$ (B)

Solve by substitution. Substitute equation (B) into equation (A).

$$\dfrac{3u}{2} + u = 15$$

Multiply all three terms by 2. Then solve for "u".

$$2 \cdot \dfrac{3u}{2} + 2 \cdot u = 2 \cdot 15$$
$$3u + 2u = 30$$
$$5u = 30$$
$$u = 6$$

Substitute u = 6 in equation (A).

$$t + u = 15$$
$$t + 6 = 15$$
$$t = 9$$

Check:

$t + u = 15$	$t = \dfrac{3u}{2}$
$9 + 6 = 15$	$9 = \dfrac{3 \cdot 6}{2}$
$15 \overset{\checkmark}{=} 15$	$9 = \dfrac{18}{2}$
	$9 \overset{\checkmark}{=} 9$

The solution is 96.

Always be sure to check you solution!

Solve these digit problems.

1. The sum of the digits of a two-digit number is 12. If the digits are interchanged, the number is increased by 36. Find the number.

2. A three-digit number has a 2 for its tens digit. The sum of the digits is 7 and the number is 31 times the units digit. Find the number.

3. In two-digit number, the units digit is 5 more than the tens digit. Three times the tens digit is 1 less than the units digit. Find the number.

4. The sum of the digits in a two-digit number is 15. If the digits are reversed, the number is decreased by 27. What is the number?

5. The sum of the digits of a two-digit number is 11. If the digits are reversed, the number is increased by 45. What is the original number?

6. If 18 is added to a two-digit number, the digits are reversed. The sum of the digits is 16. Find the original number.

7. A number is 8 times the sum of its digits. The tens digit is 5 greater than the units digit. Find the number.

8. A number between 300 and 400 is 40 times the sum of its digits. The tens digit is 6 more than the units digit. Find the number.

9. The sum of a three-digit number is 9 and the tens digit is 1 more than the hundreds digit. When the digits are reversed, the new number is 99 less than the original number. Find the original number.

10. The sum of the digits of a two-digit number is 6. If the digits are reversed, the number is decreased by 36. Find the original number.

11. The sum of the digits of a two-digit number is 13. If the number represented by reversing the digits is subtracted from the original number, the result is 27. Find the original number.

12. The sum of the digits of a two-digit number is 8. If the digits are reversed, the number is increased by 54. Find the original number.

LESSON 57 – Story Problems
Business

Example 1:   Six bars of soap and five cans of cleanser cost $3.50 At that same store, three cans of cleanser and two bars of soap cost $1.70. How much does one bar of soap and one can of cleanser cost?

Solution:

Let s = soap
Let c = cleanser

6s + 5c = 3.50   (A)
2s + 3c = 1.70   (B)

Solve by elimination. Multiply equation (B) by (–3).

–3(2s + 3c = 1.70)
–6s – 9c = –5.10

Eliminate "s" and solve for "c".

$$6s + 5c = 3.50$$
$$\underline{-6s - 9c = -5.10}$$
$$-4c = -1.60$$
$$c = 0.40$$

Substitute "c" into equation (B). Solve for "s".

2s + 3c = 1.70
2s + 3(0.40) = 1.70
2s + 1.20 = 1.70
2s = 0.50
s = 0.25

Check: 6s + 5c = 3.50   2s + 3c = 1.70
6(0.25) + 5(0.40) = 3.50   2(0.25) + 3(0.40) = 1.70
1.50 + 2.00 = 3.50   0.50 + 1.20 = 1.70
3.50 ✓ 3.50   1.70 ✓ 1.70

Solution: one can of cleanser: $0.40
one bar of soap: $0.25

Example 2:   A coat sells for $70. What is the store's cost if the selling price represents a 40% profit?

Solution: Let x = cost of the coat

x + 40%(x) = 70
x + 0.40x = 70
1.40x = 70
x = 50

Check: x + 40%(x) = 70
50 + 0.40(50) = 70
50 + 20 = 70
$70 \overset{\checkmark}{=} 70$

The store's cost of the coat is $50.

Example 3:   A farmer bought a number of sheep for $440. After 5 died, he sold the remaining sheep at a $2 profit each. However, he made a $60 profit for his dealings. How many sheep did the farmer originally buy?

Solution: Let n = number of sheep
Let r = cost of each sheep

$n \cdot r = 440$ (A)
$(n - 5)(r + 2) = 500$ (B)

Using FOIL, expand equation (B).

$nr - 5r + 2n - 10 = 500$ (C)

Substitute "nr" in equation (C). Simplify.

$440 - 5r + 2n - 10 = 500$
$-5r + 2n + 430 = 500$
$2n - 5r - 70 = 0$ (D)

Solve equation (A) for "n".

$n \cdot r = 440$
$n = \dfrac{440}{r}$

Substitute "n" in equation (D).

$$2n - 5r - 70 = 0$$

$$2\left(\frac{440}{r}\right) - 5r - 70 = 0$$

Multiply all terms by "r" to remove the fraction.

$$r \cdot 2\left(\frac{440}{r}\right) - r \cdot (5r) - r \cdot (70) = r \cdot 0$$

$2(440) - 5r^2 - 70r = 0$

$880 - 5r^2 - 70r = 0$ Multiply by –1.

$5r^2 + 70r - 880 = 0$ Divide by 5.

$r^2 + 14r - 176 = 0$

Solve the quadratic by factoring.

$r^2 + 14r - 176 = 0$

$(r + 22)(r - 8) = 0$

$r + 22 = 0$ $r - 8 = 0$

$r = -22$ $r = 8$

Since "r" represents the cost of each sheep, –22 is not a possible solution. Therefore the cost of each sheep is $8.

Substitute r = 8 in equation (A).

$n \cdot r = 440$

$n \cdot 8 = 440$

$n = 55$

The farmer originally bought 55 sheep.

Solve these business problems.

1. Lenny spent $8.40 for several pencils costing 20¢ each and some notebooks costing $1.20 each. He bought 7 more pencils than notebooks. How many notebooks did he buy?

2. Sherry worked after school weekdays at $7 per hour and on Saturday she makes $1\frac{1}{2}$ her weekday pay per hour. Sherry made $101.50 last week, working a total of 12 hours. How many hours did she work on Saturday?

3. Hector purchases some one-cent stamps, some seventeen-cent stamps and some forty-four cent stamps for $6.48. There are three times as many one-cent stamps as forty-four cent stamps and 8 fewer forty-four cent stamps then seventeen-cent stamps. How many stamps in all does he buy?

4. Each of the 24 members of the Boosters' Club bought either a $12 pennant or $18 cap for the baseball game. If the total bill was $384, how many boosters' bought pennants?

5. Seven cans of corn and three cans of peas cost $6.10 at the store. Someone else bought four cans of corn and three cans of peas for $4.45 at the same store within 20 minutes. How much did a can of corn and a can of peas cost?

6. Adult tickets for the senior class play were $6 each and student tickets were $3 each. A total of 1500 tickets worth $7200 were sold. How many adult and student tickets were sold?

7. A plumber makes $15 per hour more than an apprentice. During an 8-hour day, their earnings total $920. How much does each make per hour?

LESSON 58 – Story Problems
Age

Example 1: Jack is 20 years older than Felix. Five years ago, Jack was five times as old as Felix was then. Find the present age of Jack and Felix.

Solution:
Let   x = Felix's present age
          x + 20 = Jack's present age
          x – 5 = Felix's age five years ago
          x + 15 = Jack's age five years ago

Write an equation and solve.

Jack's age five years ago = 5 • (Felix's age five years ago)

$x + 15 = 5(x - 5)$
$x + 15 = 5x - 25$
$40 = 4x$
$10 = x$

Solution: Felix's present age is 10 and Jack's present age is 30.

Example 2: Susan is now eight years old and Michelle is two years old. In how many years will Susan be twice as old as Michelle?

Solution:

	Present Age	Age in "x" Years
Susan	8	8 + x
Michelle	2	2 + x

$8 + x = 2(2 + x)$
$8 + x = 4 + 2x$
$4 = x$

Check:
$8 + x = 2(2 + x)$
$8 + 4 = 2(2 + 4)$
$12 = 2(6)$
$12 \overset{\checkmark}{=} 12$

Solution: In 4 years, Susan will be twice as old as Michelle.

Solve these age problems.

1. Arnie is thirteen years older than Andy. The sum of their ages is 27. How old are they?

2. Peter is six years older than Bart. In five years, Peter will be twice as old as Bart. How old are they now?

3. Mack is one year older than Dave. Last year their ages added to 49. How old is each now?

4. The sum of the ages of Sue and her dog is now 18 years. In four years, the dog will be $\frac{1}{5}$ as old as Sue. How old is each now?

5. Lynda's age plus Alan's age is 32 years. The difference between twice Alan's age and $\frac{1}{2}$ Lynda's age is 29 years. Howl old is each?

6. Two years ago, Gary was twice as old as Leslie. In four years, the sum of their ages will be 30. How old are they now?

7. Last year Matilda was three times as old as Matty. In three years, she will be one year more than twice as old as Matty. How old are they now?

8. Mary is older than Bob. The differences of their ages is 8 and the sum of their ages is 60. Find the age of each.

9. In 1948, the Tyler McCloud Bridge was ten times as old as the Pittsford Bridge. That same year, the differences in their ages was 54 years. Find the year of completion for each bridge.

10. Sheila's mother is twice as old as Sheila is. Eleven years ago she was three times as old as Sheila was. Find Sheila's present age.

11. Alex is $\frac{3}{4}$ as old as Jack. Six years ago, Alex was $\frac{1}{2}$ as old as Jack. How old is each?

LESSON 59 – Story Problems
Mixture

Example 1: A solution of oil and gasoline is 8% oil. How much gasoline must be added to 3 gallons of the solution to obtain a new solution that is 5% oil?

Solution:

	Percent of oil (%)	×	Amount of mixture (gallons)	=	Amount of oil
original solution	8	×	3	=	0.08(3)
gasoline added	0	×	x	=	0
new solution	5	×	3 + x	=	0.05(3 + x)

$0.08(3) + 0 = 0.05(3 + x)$

$0.08(3) = 0.05(3 + x)$ multiply both sides by 100

$8(3) = 5(3 + x)$

$24 = 15 + 5x$

$9 = 5x$

$\dfrac{9}{5} = x$

Check it: $\dfrac{0.24}{3 + 1.8} = \dfrac{0.24}{4.8} = 0.05 \times 100 = 5\%$

Solution: $\dfrac{9}{5} = 1.8$ gallons of gasoline

Example 2: How many pounds of nuts worth 45¢ per pound must be mixed with 20 pound of nuts worth 60¢ per pound to make a mixture which can be sold at 50¢ per pound?

Solution:

	Number of pounds	×	Cost per pound (¢)	=	Value of mixture
cheap nuts	x	×	45	=	45x
better nuts	20	×	60	=	20(60)
mixture	x + 20	×	50	=	50(x + 20)

$45x + 20(60) = 50(x + 20)$

$45x + 1200 = 50x + 1000$

$200 = 5x$

$40 = x$

Check: $45x + 20(60) = 50(x + 20)$

$45(40) + 20(60) = 50(40 + 20)$

$1800 + 1200 = 2000 + 1000$

$3000 \overset{\checkmark}{=} 3000$

Solution: Need 40 pounds of 45¢ nuts.

Example 3: How much pure copper must be added to 150 pounds of an alloy which is 40% copper to produce an alloy which is 50% copper?

Solution:

	Number of pounds	×	Part pure copper (%)	=	Number of pounds of pure copper
original alloy	150	×	40	=	0.40(150)
pure copper added	n	×	100	=	1.00n
new alloy	150 + n	×	50	=	0.50(150 + n)

$0.40(150) + 1.00n = 0.50(150 + n)$

$40(150) + 100n = 50(150 + n)$ multiply both sides by 100

$6000 + 100n = 7500 + 50n$

$50n = 1500$

$n = 30$

Check: $0.40(150) + 1.00n = 0.50(150 + n)$

$0.40(150) + 1.00(30) = 0.50(150 + 30)$

$60 + 30 = 0.50(180)$

$90 \overset{\checkmark}{=} 90$

Solution: 30 pound of pure copper must be added.

Example 4: A chemist has 160 pints of a solution which is 20% acid. How much water must she evaporate to make a solution which is 40% acid?

Solution:

	Number of pints	×	Part pure acid (%)	=	Number of pints of pure acid
original solution	160	×	20	=	0.20(160)
water evaporated	x	×	0	=	0(x)
new solution	160 − x	×	40	=	0.40(160 − x)

$0.20(160) + 0(x) = 0.40(160 - x)$

$20(160) + 0 = 40(160 - x)$ multiply both sides by 100

$$3200 = 6400 - 40x$$
$$40x = 3200$$
$$x = 80$$

Solution: 80 pints of water needs to be evaporated.

Solve these mixture problems.

1.   A food store mixes dried apples costing $6 per pound with dried apricots costing $8 per pound to produce a 20 pound mixture worth $7.20 per pound. How many pounds of each are needed to produce a 20-pound mixture?

2.   A chemist mixes together 20 L of a solution that is 60% acid and 30 L of a solution that is 20% acid. What is the acid percentage of the mixture?

3.   In a science lab, 800 grams of a 15% salt solution is mixed with salt to make a solution that is 20% salt solution. How much salt was added?

4.   A grocer mixes together four pounds of peanuts costing $2 per pound with two pounds of walnuts costing $5 per pound. What should be the price per pound of this mixture?

5.   How many grams of water must be added to 50 grams of a 30% acid solution in order to produce a 20% acid solution?

6.   How many pounds of salt must be added to 30 pounds of a 20% salt solution in order to increase the salt content to 25%?

7.   Pure acid and water are mixed to produce 8 L of a solution that is 40% acid. How much of each are mixed?

8.   Cashew nuts sell for $7 per pound while peanuts sell for $2.85 per pound. A ten-pound mixture is to be made which sells for $4.51 per pound. How many pounds of each are needed to make the mixture?

9.   How many quarts of 1% milk must be added to 50 quarts of 6% butterfat milk to obtain milk that has 2% butterfat?

10.   How many kilograms of water must be evaporated from 12 kg of a 20% salt solution to produce a 60% solution?

LESSON 60 – Story Problems
Work

Example 1: Joan can paint her bedroom in six hours. With help from her brother, Joe, they paint that same bedroom in two hours. How long does it take Joe to paint the bedroom working alone?

Solution: Let "x" be the time required for Joe to paint the bedroom.

Joan's time + Joe's time = Time working together

$$\frac{1}{6} + \frac{1}{x} = \frac{1}{2}$$

Multiply all three terms by the LCD, which is 6x.

$$\frac{\cancel{6}x \cdot 1}{\cancel{6}} + \frac{6 * 1}{\cancel{x}} = \frac{\overset{3}{\cancel{6}}x \cdot 1}{\cancel{2}}$$

$$x + 6 = 3x$$
$$6 = 2x$$
$$3 = x$$

Solution: It takes Joe 3 hours to paint the bedroom.

Example 2: Bob mows the yard at his house in seven hours. When his son, Jake, does the mowing, he only takes five hours. If they work together to mow the yard, how long will it take them?

Solution: Let "x" represents working together.

$$\frac{1}{7} + \frac{1}{5} = \frac{1}{x}$$

Multiply all three terms by the LCD, 35x (7 • 5 • x).

$$\frac{\overset{5}{\cancel{35}}x \cdot 1}{\cancel{7}} + \frac{\overset{7}{\cancel{35}} * 1}{\cancel{5}} = \frac{35 * 1}{\cancel{x}}$$

$$5x + 7x = 35$$
$$12x = 35$$
$$x = \frac{35}{12} = 2\frac{11}{12} = 2 \text{ hrs } 55 \text{ min}$$

Solution: It takes 2 hrs 55 min to mow the yard together.

Example 3: If the intake pipe of a tank can fill it in three hours while it takes eight hours to drain the tank, how long will it take to fill the tank if both intake and drain pipes are open?

Solution:

$$\frac{1}{3} - \frac{1}{8} = \frac{1}{x}$$

Multiply by the common denominator: 24x

$$\frac{^8\cancel{24} \times 1}{\cancel{3}} - \frac{^3\cancel{24} \times 1}{\cancel{8}} = \frac{24 * 1}{\cancel{x}}$$

$8x - 3x = 24$

$5x = 24$

$x = \dfrac{24}{5} = 4\frac{4}{5} = 4.8 = 4$ hours 48 minutes

Check:

$$\frac{1}{3} - \frac{1}{8} = \frac{1}{\frac{24}{5}}$$

$$\frac{8}{24} - \frac{3}{24} = \frac{5}{24}$$

$$\frac{5}{24} \overset{\checkmark}{=} \frac{5}{24}$$

$$\frac{1 \times \dfrac{5}{24}}{\dfrac{24}{5} \times \dfrac{5}{24}} = \frac{\dfrac{1}{1} \times \dfrac{5}{24}}{\dfrac{24}{5} \times \dfrac{5}{24}} = \frac{\dfrac{5}{24}}{1} = \frac{5}{24}$$

Solution: It takes 4 hours 48 minutes to fill the tank.

Solve these work problems.

1. Arnie can do a job in 30 minutes. Barney can do it in 40 minutes and Carney can do it in 60 minutes. Working together, how long will it take them to do the job?

2. Candy can rake our lawn in 90 minutes and I can do it in 60 minutes. If Candy rakes for 15 minutes before I join her, how long will it take us to finish?

3. A pipe can fill a swimming pool in 6 hours. After it has been filling the empty pool for 3 hours, a second pipe is used. The result is the pool is filled in another two hours. How long will it take the second pipe alone to fill the pool?

4. Millie and Molly are addressing invitations to the junior prom. Millie can address one every 30 seconds while Molly can do one every 40 seconds. How long will it take them to address 140 invitations?

5. Jane can make a quilt in 9 days. If Didi helps her, they can make the quilt in 6 days. How long does it take Didi to make the quilt alone?

6. The fill pipe for a tank can fill the tank in 4 hours and the drain pipe can drain it in 2 hours. If both pipes are opened, how long will it take to empty a half-filled tank?

7. Gerry takes one hour to milk his herd of cows and it takes Geraldine $1\frac{1}{2}$ hours to do the same job. How long will it take both to milk the herd?

8. Stanley can load his truck in 40 minutes. If I help him it takes us 15 minutes. How long will it take me alone?

9. Pedro usually takes 50 minutes to groom the horses. After working for 10 minutes, he was joined by Martina and finished the grooming in 15 minutes. Working alone, how long would it take Martina?

10. Inez can paint her living room in 6 hours. If Hilda helps her, they can complete the job in 3 hours. How long would it take Hilda to complete the job working alone?

LESSON 61 – Story Problems
Investment

Example 1: $500 is deposited at a local savings bank that pays $4\frac{1}{4}\%$ interest per year. How much interest is earned in six months? Round answer to the nearest cent.

Solution: I = PRT Interest = Principal × Rate × Time

Put all percents over 100: $4\frac{1}{4}\% = 4.25\% = \frac{4.25}{100}$

Since the rate is per year, convert 6 months to part of a year: 6 months = $\frac{1}{2}$ year.

$$I = \$500 \times 4.25\% \times 6 \text{ months}$$

$$I = 500 \times \frac{4.25}{100} \times \frac{1}{2}$$

$$I = \frac{\overset{5}{\cancel{500}}}{1} \times \frac{4.25}{\underset{1}{\cancel{100}}} \times \frac{1}{2} = \frac{21.25}{2} = 10.625 = 10.63$$

Solution: $10.63 interest in 6 months

Example 2: If $20,000 is invested at two different interest rates, 5% and 6%, and $1120 interest is received from both rates, how much is invested at each rate?

Solution: (Interest at 5%) + (Interest at 6%) = (Total Interest)

Let "x" = amount invested at 5%.
Let "20,000 – x" = amount invested at 6%.

$$5\%(x) + 6\%(20{,}000 - x) = 1120$$
$$0.05x + 0.06(20{,}000 - x) = 1120 \quad \text{multiply both sides by 100}$$
$$5x + 6(20{,}000 - x) = 112{,}000$$
$$5x + 120{,}000 - 6x = 112{,}000$$
$$-x = -8000$$
$$x = 8000$$
$$20{,}000 - x = 12{,}000$$

Check:
$$5\%(x) + 6\%(20{,}000 - x) = 1120$$
$$400 + 720 = 1120$$
$$1120 \overset{\checkmark}{=} 1120$$

Solution: $8000 at 5% and $12,000 at 6%

Example 3: How long does it take a $5000 investment to earn $860 interest if the rate is 8% and not compounded?

Solution: $PRT = I$

$$\$5000 \times 8\% \times T = \$860$$

$$\overset{50}{\cancel{5000}} \times \frac{8}{\underset{1}{\cancel{100}}} \times T = 860$$

$$50 \times 8 \times T = 860$$
$$400T = 860$$
$$T = \frac{860}{400} = \frac{43}{20} = 2\tfrac{3}{20}$$

Check: $\$5000 \times 8\% \times T = \$860$

$$5000 \times \frac{8}{100} \times 2\tfrac{3}{20} = 860$$

$$5000 \times \frac{2}{25} \times \frac{43}{20} = 860$$

$$200 \times 2 \times \frac{43}{20} = 860$$

$$400 \times \frac{43}{20} = 860$$

$$20 \times 43 = 860$$

$$860 \overset{\checkmark}{=} 860$$

Solution: $2\tfrac{3}{20}$ years

Solve these investment problems.

1. How long does it take a $2000 investment to earn $500 interest if the interest rate is 8% per year?

2. $500 is deposited at $6\tfrac{1}{2}\%$ interest per year. How much interest is earned in 3 months?

3. You borrow $2000 for six months at an interest rate of 1.5% per month. How much interest is owed after the six months?

4. Harriet invests $6000. Some of the money is invested in stocks paying 6% a year and some in bonds paying 11% a year. She receives $580 each year from these investments. How much is invested in stocks and how much in bonds?

5. The income from stocks and bonds was equal yet $2000 more was invested in stocks. Bonds paid 7.2% interest while stocks paid 6%. How much annual income was received?

6. Bob Trooper invested half his money at 12% interest, one-third at 11% and the rest at 9%. If the total annual income is $1340, how much did Bob invest?

7. If a $2000 investment earns $180 interest in one year, find the rate of interest for one year.

8. A bank has a total of $42,000 invested in two small businesses. At the end of the year, the bank earned 12% interest on one business but lost $10\frac{1}{2}$% on the second business. If the bank's net profit was $990, how much was invested at each rate?

LESSON 62 – Story Problems
Numbers

Example 1:   The larger of two numbers is three more than twice the smaller. Their sum is 39. Find both numbers.

Solution: Let "n" = smaller number (the one you know the least about)
Let "2n + 3" = larger number

smaller number + larger number = 39
$n + 2n + 3 = 39$
$3n + 3 = 39$
$3n = 36$
$n = 12$
$2n + 3 = 2(12) + 3 = 24 + 3 = 27$

Check: $n + 2n + 3 = 39$
$12 + 2(12) + 3 = 39$
$12 + 24 + 3 = 39$
$39 \overset{\checkmark}{=} 39$

Solution: 12 and 27

Example 2:   Find three consecutive even integers such that the sum of the first and third exceeds one-half of the second by 15.

Solution: Let "n" = first integer.
Let "n + 2" = second integer.
Let "n + 4" = third integer.

first integer + third integer = $\frac{1}{2}$(second integer) + 15
$n + n + 4 = \frac{1}{2}(n + 2) + 15$
$2n + 4 = \frac{1}{2}n + 1 + 15$
$2n + 4 = \frac{1}{2}n + 16$
$\frac{3}{2}n = 12$ multiply both sides by $\frac{2}{3}$ (reciprocal of $\frac{3}{2}$)
$n = 8$
$n + 2 = 10$
$n + 4 = 12$

Check: $n + n + 4 = \frac{1}{2}(n + 2) + 15$

$8 + 12 = \frac{1}{2}(10) + 15$

$20 = 5 + 15$

$20 \overset{\checkmark}{=} 20$

Solution: 8, 10, and 12

Example 3:   What is the number that when added to both the numerator and denominator of $\frac{16}{34}$, the new fraction equals $\frac{4}{7}$?

Solution: Let "n" = the number.

$$\frac{16 + n}{34 + n} = \frac{4}{7} \qquad \text{cross multiply}$$

$7(16 + n) = 4(34 + n)$

$112 + 7n = 136 + 4n$

$3n = 24$

$n = 8$

Check: $\dfrac{16 + n}{34 + n} = \dfrac{4}{7}$

$\dfrac{16 + 8}{34 + 8} = \dfrac{4}{7}$

$\dfrac{24}{42} = \dfrac{4}{7}$

$\dfrac{4}{7} \overset{\checkmark}{=} \dfrac{4}{7}$

Solution: 8

Solve these number problems.

1.   The sum of the least and greatest of three consecutive integers is 44. What is the middle integer?

2.   Find three consecutive odd integers such that the sum of the greatest and twice the least is 25.

3.   Find four consecutive integers such that five times the third decreased by twice the fourth is 55.

4. Find three consecutive integers whose sum is −171.

5. Find three consecutive odd integers such that the greatest is 15 less than twice the smallest.

6. The two adjacent sides of a rectangle are consecutive odd integers. The perimeter is 96 inches. What are the dimensions of the rectangle?

7. Find two consecutive integers such that the lesser number increased by twice the greater is 50.

8. Find two consecutive even integers if twice the lesser integer is 16 more than the greater.

9. An odd integer is added to three times the next consecutive odd integer. If the sum is 66, find the two odd integers.

10. If the sum of three consecutive odd integers is decreased by 130, the result is equal to the second odd integer. Find the three integers.

11. Find four consecutive odd integers if the product of the two smaller integers is 80 less than the product of the two larger integers.

12. Find three consecutive even integers if the square of the third less the square of the first is equal to 128.

13. The sum of the squares of three consecutive positive integers is 110. Find the integers.

LESSON 63 – Story Problems
Inequalities

Inequality problems usually have these key words: "at least", "no more than", "at most" and "no less than". We need to be able to translate these phrases into math symbols.

Example 1:   Three added to two times a positive integer is at most 15. Find all the integers and the largest possible answer that will satisfy the criteria.

Solution: Let "n" = integer.

Symbolically, "at most" is "$\leq$".

The inequality is: $2n + 3 \leq 15$

$2n + 3 \leq 15$ subtract 3
$2n \leq 12$ divide by 2
$n \leq 6$

All possible integers are: $1 \leq x \leq 6$

Solution: $n = \{1, 2, 3, 4, 5, 6\}$ and the largest positive integer is 6.

Example 2:   The sum of two consecutive integers is no less than 61. Find the smallest pair of numbers.

Solution: Let "n" = first integer.
Let "n + 1" = second integer.

Symbolically, "no less than" is "$\geq$".

The inequality is: first integer + second integer $\geq$ 61

$n + n + 1 \geq 61$
$2n + 1 \geq 61$ subtract 1
$2n \geq 60$ divide by 2
$n \geq 30$

All pairs of consecutive integers beginning with 30.

Solution: The smallest pair of integers is 30 and 31.

Example 3: Three times the sum of 8 and a number is at least 93. Find the smallest possible number.

Solution: Let "n" = number.

Symbolically, "at least" is "≥".

The inequality is: 3(8 + number) ≥ 93

$$3(8 + n) \geq 93$$
$$24 + 3n \geq 93$$
$$3n \geq 69$$
$$n \geq 23$$

Solution: The smallest possible number is 23.

Example 4: The sum of two consecutive odd numbers is less than 46. Find the pair with the largest sum.

Solution: Let "n" = first number.

Let "n + 2" = second number

Symbolically, "less than" or "no more than" is "≤"

The inequality is: n + n + 2 ≤ 46

$$n + n + 2 \leq 46$$
$$2n + 2 \leq 46$$
$$2n \leq 44$$
$$n \leq 22$$

Note that the largest **_odd_** number is 21. The next consecutive odd number is 23. Together, their sum (44) is less than 46.

Solution: The pair with the largest sum and fits the criteria of two consecutive odd numbers is 21 and 23.

READ EACH QUESTION CAREFULLY!!!

Solve these inequality problems.

1. A rectangular piece of cloth is $3\frac{1}{2}$ feet wide. Find the maximum length possible if the area is to be at most 42 square ft (ft^2).

2. The sum of three consecutive integers is greater than 54. Find the smallest integers for which this is possible.

3. Two high-speed trains pass each other and continue in opposite directions. One train travels at 120 mph and the other at 135 mph. How long must they travel to be at least 340 miles apart?

4. Sarah received 78, 85, 70, and 83 on four tests. What is the lowest score she can make on the fifth test to average at least 80?

5. Find three consecutive even integers such that the sum of the two larger integers is less than three times the first.

6. The average of six consecutive integers is less than 15. What are the largest values possible for the integers?

7. If 3 is added to four times an integer, the sum is less than 15. What is the largest integer for which this is possible?

8. Four times the sum of 5 and twice a number is greater than or equal to 100. What is the smallest value possible for this number?

9. The sum of the digits of a two-digit number is 7. This number is greater than twice the number obtained by reversing the digits. Find the smallest possible value for the original number.

LESSON 64 – Story Problems
Percents

Example 1: What is 80% of 60?

Solution: $\dfrac{\text{Percent}}{100} = \dfrac{\text{Part}}{\text{Whole}}$

Let "N" = part.

$\dfrac{80}{100} = \dfrac{N}{60}$ cross multiply

100N = 80(60)
100N = 4800
N = 48

Solution: 48

Example 2: 16 is part percent of 40?

Solution: $\dfrac{\text{Percent}}{100} = \dfrac{\text{Part}}{\text{Whole}}$

Let "N" = percent.

$\dfrac{N}{100} = \dfrac{16}{40}$ cross multiply

40N = 16(100)
40N = 1600
N = 40

Solution: 40%

Example 3: 12 is 30% of what?

Solution: $\dfrac{\text{Percent}}{100} = \dfrac{\text{Part}}{\text{Whole}}$

Let "N" = whole.

$\dfrac{30}{100} = \dfrac{12}{N}$ cross multiply

$$30N = 12(100)$$
$$30N = 1200$$
$$N = 40$$

Solution: 40

Example 4:   Tom bought an I-Pod for $300, which was a discount of 25%. What was the original price?

Solution: Rephrase the question! If the discount was 25%, how much was actually paid?

The new question would be: $300 = 75% of what number?

$$\frac{Percent}{100} = \frac{Part}{Whole}$$

Let "N" = original price.

$$\frac{75}{100} = \frac{300}{N} \quad \text{cross multiply}$$
$$75N = 300(100)$$
$$75N = 30000$$
$$N = 400$$

Solution: The original price is $400.

Solve these percent problems.

1.   Last year, Polly earned $18,000. How much was the raise if it was a 12%?

2.   3.75 is 60% of what number?

3.   A $60 sweater is on sale for $48. What is the percent of decrease?

4.   The annual membership fee in the computer club increased from $30 to $36. What was the percent increase?

5. Elaine bought 100 shares of stock at $25 per share and sold them at $31 per share. What was her percent profit?

6. What percent of 300 is 75?

7. A family's monthly rent is 18% of their monthly income. If the rent is $360, how much is the monthly income?

8. The price of a gallon of paint that normally sells for $9.80 is reduced 35%. How much is the new price?

9. Bob Jones received a 15% commission for selling furniture. If the commission was $150, what was the selling price of the furniture?

10. How many minutes of commercial time does Waverly have during a half-hour TV program that uses 20% of time for commercials if it gets $33\frac{1}{3}$% of commercial time?

11. The price of a refrigerator was reduced from $520 to $416. Find the percent of discount.

12. The sticker price for a new car is $6696. This includes the optional items which are 24% of the base price. Find the base price.

13. 44 is 110% of what number?

14. 12 is what percent of 96?

15. What is 60% of 240?

LESSON 65 – Story Problems
Geometry

Example 1:   The longer side of a rectangle exceeds the shorter by six feet. If we decrease the longer side by three feet and increase the shorter side by two feet, the areas of both rectangles will be equal. Find the dimensions of the original rectangle.

Solution: $A = LW$

Let "x" = shorter side of original rectangle.

	longer side	•	shorter side	=	Area
original rectangle	$x + 6$	•	x	=	$x(x + 6)$
new rectangle	$x + 3$	•	$x + 2$	=	$(x + 3)(x + 2)$

Area of original rectangle = Area of new rectangle

$$x(x + 6) = (x + 3)(x + 2) \quad \text{expand each side}$$
$$x^2 + 6x = x^2 + 5x + 6 \quad x^2 \text{ terms cancel out}$$
$$6x = 5x + 6$$
$$x = 6$$
$$x + 6 = 12$$

Solution: The dimensions of the original rectangle are 12 ft by 6 ft.

Example 2:   The area of a rectangle is 28 square feet while its perimeter is 22 feet. Find the dimensions of the rectangle.

Solution: $A = LW$ (i)
$P = 2(L + W)$ (ii)

Let "L" = length of rectangle.
Let "W" = width of rectangle.

Solve equation (ii) for "L"

$$2(L + W) = P$$
$$2(L + W) = 22 \quad \text{divide by 2}$$
$$L + W = 11 \quad \text{solve for "L"}$$
$$L = 11 - W$$

Substitute into equation (i).

$$A = LW$$
$$28 = (11 - W)(W)$$
$$28 = 11W - W^2$$
$$0 = -28 + 11W - W^2 \qquad \text{multiply through by } -1$$
$$0 = 28 - 11W + W^2$$
$$0 = (7 - W)(4 - W)$$

$$0 = 7 - W \qquad\qquad 0 = 4 - W$$
$$W = 7 \qquad\qquad\quad W = 4$$

Substitute into equation (ii).

$$P = 2(L + W) \qquad\qquad P = 2(L + W)$$
$$22 = 2(L + 7) \qquad\qquad 22 = 2(L + 4)$$
$$22 = 2L + 14 \qquad\qquad 22 = 2L + 8$$
$$8 = 2L \qquad\qquad\qquad 14 = 2L$$
$$4 = L \qquad\qquad\qquad\; 7 = L$$

Solution: There are two solutions!

Length = 4 ft, Width = 7 ft
and
Length = 7 ft, Width = 4 ft

Example 3:   The width of a concrete walk around a 28 ft by 14 ft swimming pool is two feet. What is the area of this concrete walk?

Solution: We need to find the dimensions of the larger rectangle and then subtract the area of the swimming pool to arrive at the area of the concrete walk.

Area of the larger rectangle – Area of swimming pool = Area of walk

$$(28 + 4)(14 + 4) - (28)(14) =$$
$$(32)(18) - (28)(14) =$$
$$576 - 392 =$$
$$184$$

Solution: The area of the concrete walk is 184 square feet.

Solve these geometry problems.

1. Find the area of a rectangle if the perimeter of the square is 12 inches?

2. The perimeter of a rectangle is 48 inches. The width is 5 inches less than its length. Find the length of the rectangle and also its width.

3. A rectangular swimming pool is 15 feet longer than it is wide. A concrete walk 2.5 feet wide surrounds the pool. If the area of the walk is 350 ft^2, what are the dimensions of the pool?

4. If the sides of a square are doubled, the new area is 75 in.^{2} greater than the original area. Find the length of a side of the original square.

5. The length of a rectangle is 2 inches less than three times the width. Its perimeter is 52 inches. What is the width?

6. A board 20 feet long is cut into two pieces. How long is each piece if the difference between their lengths is 3 feet?

7. The length and width of a rectangle have the ratio 5:2. If the area of the rectangle is 640 square units, find the length and width.

8. One of the equal angles of an isosceles triangle measures 43°. Find the measures of the other angles.

9. Find the number of degrees in each of two supplementary angles that have measures of $(2x + 10)°$ and $(3x - 15)°$.

10. The adjacent sides of a parallelogram are respectively 10 and 12 inches. When a perpendicular line is drawn to the longer side, it measures 8 inches. Is the area of the parallelogram greater then, equal to, or less than 100 in.^{2}?

LESSON 66 – More Story Problems

Solve these story problems.

1. The product of two consecutive integers is 132. Find two pairs of numbers that satisfy this condition.

2. Two jet aircraft take off from the same airbase at the same time. One flies due north at 540 mph. The other jet flies due south at 680 mph. For how many hours will they be no more than 7320 miles apart?

3. A suit that sold for $162 is now on sale for $108. What is the percent of discount?

4. What percent of 90 is 225?

5. After a family bought a compact car, its yearly gasoline costs decreased from $600 to $450. What is the percent of decrease?

6. A square 3 inches by 3 inches is removed from a larger square. The area that remains in the larger square is 55 in.^{2}. Find the dimensions of the larger square.

7. The perimeter of a right triangle is 36 inches and one of the legs is 3 inches longer than the other. Find the lengths of the three sides.

8. Find the number of degrees in each angle of a triangle if their measurements are $(2x + 9)°$, $(x – 12)°$, and $(3x + 15)°$.

9. The sum of the digits of a two-digit number is 12. If the digits are interchanged, the number is decreased by 54. Find the number.

10. A coin collector received 79 coins and paid the seller $6.30 for the nickels and dimes. How many nickels and dimes did he receive?

11. The sum of a number and the reciprocal of three times the number is $\frac{?}{6}$. Find the number.

LESSON 67 - Functions

By definition, a set of ordered pairs or a graph is a function, if and only if, for every "x" there is a unique "y". Let us explain with examples.

Example 1:   Is the following sets of number pairs a function?

(a)   { (1, 1) , (2, 3) , (5, 7) , (9, 11) }

Since there is a unique "y" for every "x", this set of ordered pairs is a function. It can also be written this way:

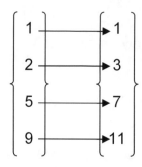

(b)   { (2, 3) , (3, 4) , (3, 5) , (6, 8) }

Because of (3, 4) and (3, 5), this set of ordered pairs is NOT a function.

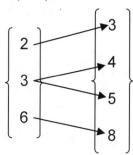

(c)   { (1, 1) , (1, 2) , (1, 3) , (1, 4) , (1, 5) }

No, this set of ordered pairs has the same "x" for five "y's". Therefore, it is NOT unique. If we were to graph these five points on a coordinate plane, it would look like the graph to the right. If we were to connect the points, a VERTICAL line would be created.

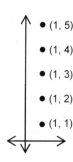

130

In all these examples, the set of ordered pairs is a relation, but examples (b) and (c) are not functions.

A Generalization: Every set of ordered pairs is a relation but not every set of ordered pairs (relation) is a function.

Example 2:   Is the equation y = 2x + 3 a function?

Solution: The equation IS a function since for every value of "x" there is a unique solution (that being "y"). Sometimes we write the equation as f(x) = 2x + 3 and it is read "f of x". If we chart this function it would look something like this:

x	2x + 3	y
0	2(0) + 3	3
1	2(1) + 3	5
2	2(2) + 3	7
3	2(3) + 3	9
−1	2(−1) + 3	1
−2	2(−2) + 3	−1
−3	2(−3) + 3	−3

No matter what number replaces "x", a unique "y" will appear. Therefore, we have a function.

Since f(x) was just introduced, we need to examine this functional notation symbolism. We may also replace f(x) with g(x), z(x), or any other letter.

$$y = x - 5$$
$$f(x) = x - 5$$
$$f(2) = 2 - 5 = -3$$
$$f(-1) = -1 - 5 = -6$$
$$f(6) = 6 - 5 = 1$$

Example 3:   Let f(x) = 2x − 5, find f(−2), f(0), f(3), and f(−6).

Solution:
$$f(-2) = 2(-2) - 5 = -4 - 5 = -9$$
$$f(0) = 2(0) - 5 = 0 - 5 = -5$$
$$f(3) = 2(3) - 5 = 6 - 5 = 1$$
$$f(-6) = 2(-6) - 5 = -12 - 5 = -17$$

Example 4:   Let $g(x) = x^3 + 2x^2 - 3$, find $g(1)$, $g(-2)$, $g(2)$, and $-g(2)$.

Solution: $g(1) = (1)^3 + 2(1)^2 - 3 = 1 + 2(1) - 3 = 1 + 2 - 3 = 0$
$g(-2) = (-2)^3 + 2(-2)^2 - 3 = -8 + 2(4) - 3 = -8 + 8 - 3 = -3$
$g(2) = (2)^3 + 2(2)^2 - 3 = 8 + 2(4) - 3 = 8 + 8 - 3 = 13$
$-g(2) = -g(-2) = -[(-2)^3 + 2(-2)^2 - 3] = -[-8 + 2(4) - 3]$
$\qquad\qquad\quad = -[-8 + 8 - 3] = -[-3] = 3$

We need to try another linear equation to show this functional property.

Example 5:   Is $y = -\frac{2}{3}x + 5$ a function?

Solution: Here is the chart and graph of the equation.

x	$-\frac{2}{3}x + 5$	y
0	$-\frac{2}{3}(0) + 5$	5
1	$-\frac{2}{3}(1) + 5$	$4\frac{1}{3}$
−1	$-\frac{2}{3}(-1) + 5$	$5\frac{2}{3}$
2	$-\frac{2}{3}(2) + 5$	$3\frac{2}{3}$
−2	$-\frac{2}{3}(-2) + 5$	$6\frac{1}{3}$
3	$-\frac{2}{3}(3) + 5$	3
−3	$-\frac{2}{3}(-3) + 5$	7
4	$-\frac{2}{3}(4) + 5$	$2\frac{1}{3}$
−4	$-\frac{2}{3}(-4) + 5$	$7\frac{2}{3}$

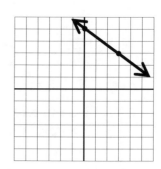

By the way, the x- and y-intercepts are as follows: (0, 5) and (7.5, 0).

The Vertical Line Test

The Vertical Line Test is another way to tell whether a graph represents a function. The depicted graph represents a function, if and only if, every vertical line intersects the graph at only one point.

Answer these questions concerning functions.

1.   Are the following sets of number pairs a function?

        a. {(1, 3), (1, 5), (1, 6), (1, 7), (1, 8)}
        b. {(2, 3), (3, 4), (4, 5), (5, 6), (6, 7)}
        c. {(8, 6), (8, 7), (8, 8), (8, 9), (8, 10)}
        d. {(−4, −2), (−2,0), (0, 2), (2, 4), (4, 6)}
        e. {(6, 1), (5, 1), (4, 1), (3, 1), (2, 1)}

2.   Is the equation, $y = 3x + 4$, a function?

3.   Is the equation, $x = 4y + 5$, a function?

4.   Let $f(x) = 3x^2 - 4$. Find the following:

        a. f(3)   c. f(1)   e. f(−1)   g. f(b)   i. f(3x)
        b. f(−2)   d. f(0)   f. f(a)   h. f(−y)   j. f(c^2)

5.   Which of these graphs is a function?

        a.   b.   c.   d.   e.   f.

6.   For each function, evaluate

                i.   f(4) − f(1)   ii. $\dfrac{f(3)}{f(2)}$ iii.   f(a^2)

        a. $f(x) = x^3 + x^2 - 3x + 4$
        b. $f(x) = 3x^2 + 12$
        c. $f(x) = -4x - 5$
        d. $f(x) = 8x^2 - 6x + 9$
        e. $f(x) = 5x - 7$

LESSON 68 – Function Within a Function and Absolute Value Functions

Several aspects of a function are discussed in this lesson. First, let us examine two distinct functions to evaluate.

Example 1:   Let $f(x) = 3x + 4$ and $h(x) = 4x - 5$. Evaluate each of the following:

a. $f(3) + h(4)$
$f(x) = 3x + 4$ $h(x) = 4x - 5$
$f(3) = 3(3) + 4 = 13$ $h(4) = 4(4) - 5 = 11$

$f(3) + h(4) = 13 + 11 = $ **24**

b. $f(-2) + h(-3)$
$f(x) = 3x + 4$ $h(x) = 4x - 5$
$f(-2) = 3(-2) + 4 = -2$ $h(-3) = 4(-3) - 5 = -17$

$f(-2) + h(-3) = -2 + (-17) = $ **–19**

c. $f(x) - h(x)$

$f(x) = 3x + 4$ $h(x) = 4x - 5$

$(3x + 4) - (4x - 5) = 3x + 4 - 4x + 5 = $ **–x + 9**

d. $f(h(2))$

$f(x) = 3x + 4$ $h(x) = 4x - 5$

$f(h(2)) = f(4(2) - 5) = f(8 - 5) = f(3)$

$f(3) = 3(3) + 4 = 9 + 4 = $ **13**

e. $h(f(-3))$

$f(x) = 3x + 4$ $h(x) = 4x - 5$

$h(f(-3)) = h(3(-3) + 4) = h(-9 + 4) = h(-5)$

$h(-5) = 4(-5) - 5 = -20 - 5 = $ **–25**

The absolute value function is described by the equation y = |x|. If you graph this function using a table of values as a guide, it looks something like the following two examples.

Example 2:   y = |x|

x	0	1	−1	2	−2	3	−3	4	−4
y	0	1	1	2	2	3	3	4	4

It's graph looks like this: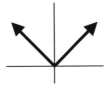

When using the vertical line test, you can see **it is a function**.

Example 3:   x = |y|

y	0	1	−1	2	−2	3	−3	4	−4
x	0	1	1	2	2	3	3	4	4

It's graph looks like this:

When using the vertical line test, you can see **it is NOT a function**.

Answer these questions concerning functions.

1.   Let f(x) = 2x + 5 and g(x) = x^2 − 4. Evaluate the following.

a.   f(3) − f(−2)   f.   f(d^2) + g(d)

b.   f(−4) + g(2)   g.   f(4) − f(5)

c.   g(−4) + f(2)   h.   g(−5) + f(2)

d.   g(3) ÷ f(−1)   i.   f(6) − g(−2)

e.   g(f(1))   j.   f(g(g(2)))

135

2. Graph each problem and indicate whether the graph represents a function.

a. $y = |x + 2|$

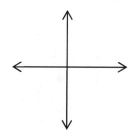

b. $y = |x - 3|$

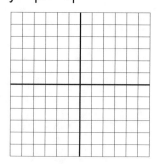

c. $x = |2y|$

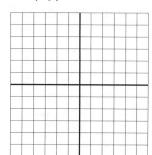

d. $x = |y|$

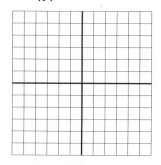

e. $y = -|x - 5|$

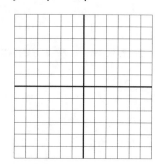

f. $x = |y + 3|$

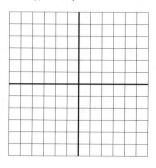

g. $y = -|2x + 1|$

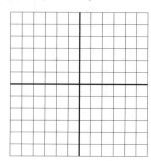

h. $x = |y - 2|$

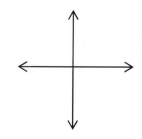

LESSON 69 – Graphing the Quadratic Equation: $y = ax^2$ and $y = ax^2 + k$

The graph of a linear equation, $y = mx + b$ or $ax + by = c$, is a straight line. When we move to a quadratic equation such as $y = ax^2$, we have a curve.

The quadratic equation $y = ax^2$ passes through the origin since $y = 0$ when $x = 0$. We need to plot several points as shown in the following table:

x	−3	−2	−1	0	1	2	3
y	9	4	1	0	1	4	9

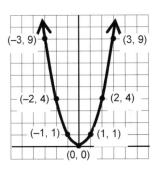

The graph of this equation is to the right. The equation $y = x^2$ defines a function and can be written $f(x) = x^2$. This graph is called a **_parabola_** with the y-axis as its axis of symmetry. As you can see from the drawing, the y-axis acts as a mirror dividing the curve into two symmetric parts. The point $(0, 0)$ is the vertex (minimum or maximum point) of the parabola. In this example, it is the minimum point of the curve, the point for which "y" has the <u>least</u> value.

The **_domain_** (the set of replacement values allowed for "x") is any real number. The **_range_**) the set of replacement values allowed for "y") consists of all non-negative numbers.

Therefore, the domain and range for $f(x) = x^2$ is

        Domain: "x" is any real number
        Range: all $y \geq 0$

In summary, the steps for graphing and finding the domain and range for the quadratic equation in the form $y = ax^2$, is:

    Step 1:   Set up a table of values.
    Step 2:   Plot the points and draw the curve.
    Step 3:   Using the graph, state the domain and range.

Example 1:   Graph $y = -x^2$ and state the domain and range.

Solution:

Step 1:

x	y
−3	−9
−2	−4
−1	−1
0	0
1	1
2	4
3	9

Step 2:

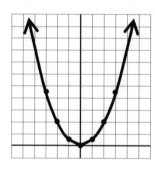

Step 3:

Domain: set of real numbers

Range: numbers that are negative or 0: $y \leq 0$

Maximum point: (0, 0)

Example 2:   Graph $y = \frac{1}{2}x^2$ and state the domain and range.

Solution:

Step 1:

x	y
−4	8
−3	9/2
−2	2
−1	12
0	0
1	1/2
2	2
3	9/2
4	8

Step 2:

Step 3:

Domain: all real numbers

Range: all non-negative numbers

Minimum point: (0, 0)

We graphed the quadratic equation $y = ax^2$ with the vertex at (0, 0). In the equation $y = ax^2 + k$, the vertex is not at (0, 0) but on either the x- or y-axis. For our purpose, the vertex will lie on the y-axis.

The steps involved are:

Step 1: Make a table of values for "x" and then solve for "y".
Step 2: Plot the points and draw a smooth graph of the parabola curve.
Step 3: Determine the domain, range, and vertex.

Example 3: $y = x^2 + 2$

Solution:

Step 1: Step 2: Step 3:

x	y
−3	11
−2	6
−1	3
0	2
1	3
2	6
3	11

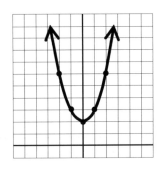

Domain: all real numbers

Range: $f(x) \geq 2$

Vertex: (0, 2), minimum point

Example 4: $y = -2x^2 + 5$

Solution:

Step 1: Step 2: Step 3:

x	y
−3	−13
−2	−3
−1	3
0	5
1	3
2	−3
3	−13

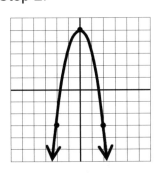

Domain: all real numbers

Range: $f(x) \leq 5$

Vertex: (0, 5), maximum point

Graphing the quadratic equations: $y = ax^2$ or $y = ax^2 + k$. Also indicate the vertex and axis of symmetry.

1. $y = 4x^2$

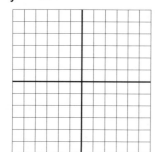

2. $y = -3x^2 + 5$

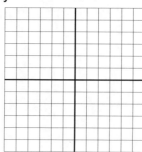

3. $y = \frac{1}{4}x^2 - 5$

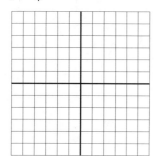

4. $y = -2x^2 + 6$

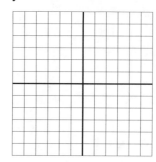

5. $y = 3x^2 - 2$

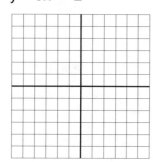

6. $y = -\frac{3}{4}x^2 + 3$

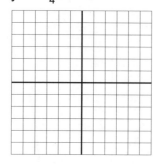

7. $y = -x^2$

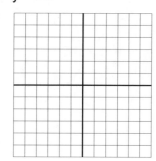

8. $y = -2x^2 + 4$

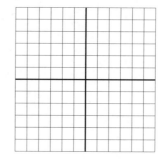

LESSON 71 – Graphing the Quadratic Equation: $y = a(x - h)^2 + k$

Previously, we graphed the quadratic equations $y = ax^2$ and $y = ax^2 + k$. We now add the quadratic equation $y = a(x - h)^2 + k$ which is graphed like the others. However, the vertex will stay on the x-axis but move left or right of (0, 0) and the axis of symmetry will be a vertical line through the vertex. Let us examine some examples.

Step 1:   Make a table of values.
Step 2:   Plot the points and draw a smooth curve.
Step 3:   Determine the domain, range, vertex and whether it is a minimum or maximum point, and the axis of symmetry.

Example 1: $y = (x - 2)^2$

Solution:

Step 1:   Step 2:   Step 3:

x	y
–1	9
0	4
1	1
2	0
3	1
4	4
5	9

Domain: all real numbers

Range: $y \geq 2$

Vertex: (3, 1), minimum point

Axis of symmetry: x = 3

Example 2: $y = (x - 3)^2 + 1$

Solution:

Step 1:   Step 2:   Step 3:

x	y
0	10
1	5
2	2
3	1
4	2
5	5

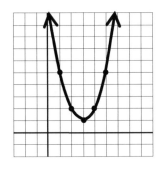

Domain: all real numbers

Range: $y \geq 0$

Vertex: (2, 0), minimum point

Axis of symmetry: x = 2

Example 3: $y = -(x + 1)^2 - 2$

Solution:

Step 1:

x	y
−4	−11
−3	−6
−2	−3
−1	−2
0	−3
1	−6

Step 2:

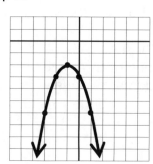

Step 3:

Domain: all real numbers

Range: $y \leq -2$

Vertex: (−1, −2), maximum point

Axis of symmetry: x = −1

Example 4: $y = 2(x - 2)^2 + 1$

Solution:

Step 1:

x	y
−2	33
−1	19
0	9
1	3
2	1
3	3
4	9

Step 2:

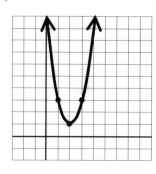

Step 3:

Domain: all real numbers

Range: $y \geq 10$

Vertex: (1, 1), minimum point

Axis of symmetry: x = 1

Graphing the quadratic equations: $y = a(x - h)^2 + k$. Also identify the domain, range, vertex, maximum or minimum point, and axis of symmetry.

1. $y = (x + 2)^2$

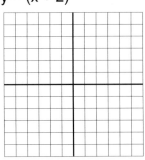

2. $y = -(x + 1)^2 - 2$

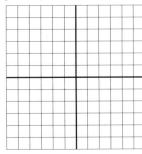

3. $y = (x - 3)^2$

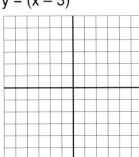
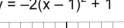

4. $y = 3(x - 2)^2 - 1$

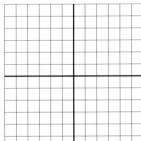

5. $y = -2(x - 1)^2 + 1$

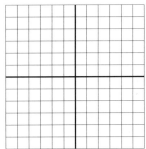

6. $y = (x - 4)^2 + 2$

7. $y = 2(x + 3)^2 - 5$

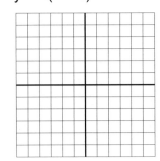

8. $y = -(x + 2)^2 + 3$

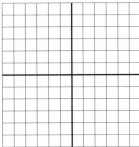

LESSON 72 – The Discriminate

Find the discriminate of any quadratic equation lets us know how many roots there are for it. The discriminate is a quantity (number) that helps us identify what type of roots the quadratic equation has. At most, any quadratic will have two roots. By finding the discriminate, we can be more precise.

Given the general form of the quadratic equation, $ax^2 + bx + c = 0$, we use the formula **$b^2 – 4ac$** to find the discriminate.

If $b^2 – 4ac > 0$, then the equation has two roots.
If $b^2 – 4ac = 0$, then the equation has one root.
If $b^2 – 4ac < 0$, then the equation has no real roots. By having **_no_** real roots, there are **_no_** x-intercepts. In other words, there are **_no_** x-values for which y = 0.

Looking at some examples, let us use the value of the discriminate to identify the number of roots for each equation.

Example 1: $x^2 – 5x – 8 = 0$

Solution: a = 1, b = –5, c = –8
$b^2 – 4ac = (–5)^2 – 4(1)(–8) = 25 + 32 = 57$
$b^2 – 4ac > 0$, therefore there are two roots.

Example 2: $x^2 + 7x + 13 = 0$

Solution: a = 1, b = 7, c = 13
$b^2 – 4ac = (7)^2 – 4(1)(13) = 49 – 52 = –3$
$b^2 – 4ac < 0$, therefore there are no real roots.

Example 3: $x^2 – 8x + 16 = 0$

Solution: a = 1, b = –8, c = 16
$b^2 – 4ac = (–8)^2 – 4(1)(16) = 64 – 64 = 0$
b2 – 4ac = 0, therefore there is one root.

Example 4: $3x^2 + x – 1 = 0$

Solution: a = 3, b = 1, c = –1
$b^2 – 4ac = (1)^2 – 4(3)(–1) = 1 + 12 = 13$
$b^2 – 4ac > 0$, therefore there are two roots.

Evaluate the discriminate to determine the number of real roots and whether the roots are rational or irrational.

1. $x^2 + 5x + 6 = 0$

2. $2x^2 + 4x - 8 = 0$

3. $-x^2 + 3x + 4 = 0$

4. $3x^2 + 8x + 9 = 0$

5. $x^2 - 8x + 16 = 0$

6. $-x^2 + 10x - 25 = 0$

7. $2x^2 - 6x + 30 = 0$

8. $4x^2 + 16x + 64 = 0$

9. $x^2 + 14x + 48 = 0$

10. $9x^2 - 12x + 4 = 0$

11. $2x^2 - 5x - 1 = 0$

12. $x^2 + 2x + 4 = 0$

13. $-x^2 = 2x - 3$

14. $3x^2 + x - 1 = 0$

15. $x^2 + 8x + 16 = 0$

16. $x^2 - 8x + 15 = 0$

LESSON 73 – The Pythagorean Theorem

Having explained various quadratic equations, both in graphing and solving, we can now practice some practical applications of the quadratic.

The Pythagorean Theorem, named after its founder, lets us examine distances of the sides of a right triangle. A drawing is very helpful in understanding this mathematical concept.

The Pythagorean Theorem is

$$a^2 + b^2 = c^2$$

where angle C ($\angle$C) is a right angle, "c" is the side opposite the right angle (called the hypotenuse), and "a" and "b" are the legs of the right triangle.

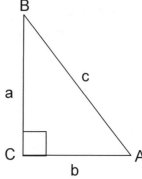

Example 1:   The hypotenuse of a right triangle is 2 inches longer than one side and 4 inches longer than the other side. Find the length of all three sides of the triangle.

Solution: Draw a triangle and label the sides and angles.

$x^2 = (x - 2)^2 + (x - 4)^2$
$x^2 = x^2 - 4x + 4 + x^2 - 8x + 16$
$x^2 = 2x^2 - 12x + 20$
$0 = x^2 - 12x + 20$
$0 = (x - 10)(x - 2)$

$x - 10 = 0$ $x - 2 = 0$
$x = 10$ $x = 2$ not a possible solution

$x - 2 = 10 - 2 = 8$
$x - 4 = 10 - 4 = 6$

Check: $(x - 2)^2 + (x - 4)^2 = x^2$
$(10 - 2)^2 + (10 - 4)^2 = (10)^2$
$8^2 + 6^2 = 10^2$
$64 + 36 = 100$
$100 \overset{\checkmark}{=} 100$

Solution: The legs of the triangle are 8 inches and 6 inches and the hypotenuse is 10 inches.

Example 2: The perimeter of a right triangle is 40 inches. If the hypotenuse is 17 inches, find the length of each of the legs.

Solution: The perimeter of the triangle minus the length of the hypotenuse is the sum of the two legs.

40 inches – 17 inches = 23 inches

$17^2 = x^2 + (23 – x)^2$
$289 = x^2 + 529 – 46x + x^2$
$289 = 2x^2 – 46x + 529$
$0 = 2x^2 – 46x + 240$
$0 = x^2 – 23x + 120$
$0 = (x – 15)(x – 8)$

x – 15 = 0   x – 8 = 0
x = 15   x = 8

Check: $15^2 + 8^2 = 17^2$
          225 + 64 = 289
          289 ≟ 289

Solution: The legs of the triangle are 15 inches and 8 inches.

Example 3: The diagonal of a rectangle is 13 feet while its perimeter is 34 feet. Find the length and width of this rectangle.

Solution: $a^2 + b2 = 13^2$ (A)
             2a + 2b = 34 (B)

Solve equation (B) for "a".

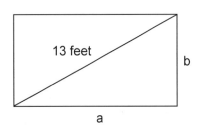

             2a + 2b = 34
             a + b = 17
             a = 17 – b (C)

Substitute equation (C) into equation (A) and solve for "b".

             $(17 – b)^2 + b^2 = 13^2$
             $289 – 34b + b^2 + b^2 = 169$
             $2b^2 – 34b + 289 = 169$
             $2b^2 – 34b + 120 = 0$
             $b^2 – 17b + 60 = 0$
             (b – 12)(b – 5) = 0

$$b - 12 = 0 \qquad b - 5 = 0$$
$$b = 12 \text{ ft} \qquad b = 5 \text{ ft}$$
$$a = 5 \text{ ft} \qquad a = 12 \text{ ft} \qquad \text{Two sets of solutions.}$$

Solve these problems using the Pythagorean Theorem.

1.   The base of a trapezoid is twice the length of its parallel side. The area of the rectangle formed within the trapezoid is 96 yd², while each right triangle's area is 24 yd². Find the perimeter of the trapezoid if its height is 8 yd. Hint: A drawing may be beneficial.

2.   In Figure 1, what is the length of BC?

3.   How far from the building in Figure 2, is the ladder?

4.   Find the area of Figure 3.

5.   Find the height of the tower in Figure 4.

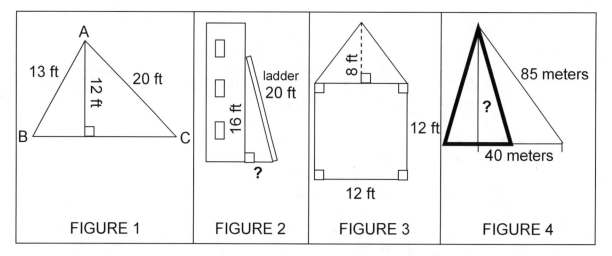

6.   Two legs of a right triangle are 7 ft and 24 ft. How long is the third side or the hypotenuse? Leave answer in simplest radical form if necessary.

7.   Find the length of a diagonal of a square 5 meters on a side.

8.   The length of three sides of a triangle are 24, 45, and 51. Can the triangle be a right triangle?

9.   Triangle ABC has a right angle at C, with AC = 32 and AB = 40. If P is on side AC such that PA = PB, find the length of these equal segments.

LESSON 74 – The Distance Formula

The distance between any two points (x_1, y_1) and (x_2, y_2) is given by the formula:

$$d = \sqrt{(x_2 - x_1)^2 + (y_2 - y_1)^2}$$

Example 1:   Find the distance between $(-2, 1)$ and $(3, 4)$.

   Solution: Let $(x_1, y_1) = (-2, 1)$ and $(x_2, y_2) = (3, 4)$.

$$d = \sqrt{(x_2 - x_1)^2 + (y_2 - y_1)^2}$$
$$d = \sqrt{(3 - (-2))^2 + (4 - 1)^2}$$
$$d = \sqrt{5^2 + 3^2}$$
$$d = \sqrt{25 + 9}$$
$$d = \sqrt{34}$$

Example 2:   Find the distance between $(3, -6)$ and $(2, 7)$.

   Solution:
$$d = \sqrt{(x_2 - x_1)^2 + (y_2 - y_1)^2}$$
$$d = \sqrt{(2 - 3)^2 + (7 - (-6))^2}$$
$$d = \sqrt{(-1)^2 + 13^2}$$
$$d = \sqrt{1 + 169}$$
$$d = \sqrt{170}$$

Example 3:   Find the perimeter of triangle ABD given A(2, 3), B(8, 3), and D(8, 5),

   Solution: $\overline{AD} = \sqrt{(5 - 3)^2 + (8 - 2)^2} = \sqrt{2^2 + 6^2} = \sqrt{40} = 2\sqrt{10}$

   $\overline{AB} = \sqrt{(8 - 2)^2 + (3 - 3)^2} = \sqrt{6^2 + 0^2} = \sqrt{6^2} = 6$

   $\overline{BD} = \sqrt{(5 - 3)^2 + (8 - 8)^2} = \sqrt{2^2 + 0^2} = \sqrt{2^2} = 2$

   Perimeter $= 6 + 2 + 2\sqrt{10} = 8 + 2\sqrt{10}$

Solve these problems using the Distance Formula.

1.   The vertices of a right triangle are at (1, 1), (1,7), and (9, 1). The right angle is at vertex (1, 1). Find the perimeter and area of the triangle.

2. A square sits inside the first and second quadrant with one location at (–5, 3) and another is at (7,3). Find its area, the other two points and length of the diagonal of the square.

3. Find the area of this figure.

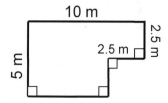

4. Find the perimeter of this figure.

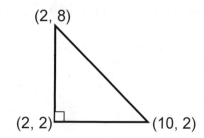

5. Find the perimeter of a quadrilateral, KLMN, with vertices at M(–2, –2), K(0, 6), N(4, 0), and L(–10, 6).

6. Find the diameter of a circle with center at (1, 2) and passing through the point (–3, 7).

7. Locate the remaining three points of a square where one right angle is at (0, 0) and the length of the side is 6 units.

8. Show that the points (1, 1), (5, 2), and (4, –2) are the vertices of an isosceles triangle.

9. What is the midpoint of a segment joining (3, 8) and (–7, –12).

LESSON 75 – Radical Equations

Radical equations contain a variable under the radical sign ($\sqrt{}$). We can solve these equations by several techniques. Here are some examples to practice and understand.

Example 1:   Solve $\sqrt{x} = 5$.

    Solution: Square both sides.

$$(\sqrt{x})^2 = 5^2$$
$$x = 25$$

    Check: $\sqrt{25} = 5$
$$5 \overset{\checkmark}{=} 5$$

    Solution: $x = 25$

Example 2:   Solve $\sqrt{x + 3} = 8$.

    Solution: Square both sides.

$$(\sqrt{x + 3})^2 = 8^2$$
$$x + 3 = 64$$
$$x = 61$$

    Check: $\sqrt{61 + 3} = 8$
$$\sqrt{64} = 8$$
$$8 \overset{\checkmark}{=} 8$$

    Solution: $x = 61$

Example 3:   Solve $\sqrt{a} + 5 = 12$

    Solution: Isolate the radical by subtracting 5 from both sides.

$$\sqrt{a} = 7$$

Square both sides.

$$(\sqrt{a})^2 = 7^2$$
$$a = 49$$

Check: $\sqrt{49} + 5 = 12$
            $7 + 5 = 12$
            $12 \overset{\checkmark}{=} 12$

Solution: a = 49

Example 4:   Solve $\sqrt{b} + 6 = 2$

Solution: Isolate the radical by subtracting 6 from both sides: $\sqrt{b} = -4$

            Square both sides: $(\sqrt{b})^2 = (-4)^2$
            $b = 16$

Check: $\sqrt{16} + 6 = 2$
            $4 + 6 = 2$
            $10 \neq 2$

Solution: Since $10 \neq 2$, there is **_no solution_** to this problem!!

BE CAREFUL!!! SOMETIMES RADICAL EQUATION <u>DO NOT</u> HAVE A SOLUTION. MAKE CERTAIN YOU CHECK YOUR WORK THOROUGHLY!!!

1. $\sqrt{b + 4} = 3$

2. $\sqrt{e} = 6$

3. $\sqrt{4b + 2} = \sqrt{b + 8}$

4. $3\sqrt{b} + 6 = 9$

5. $\sqrt{w^2} - 3 = 8$

6. $\sqrt{4 + x} = 3$

7. $\sqrt{2c} = 4$

8. $\dfrac{\sqrt{x}}{3} = 2$

9. $4\sqrt{x} + 8 = 6$

10. $\sqrt{z} = -6$

11. $3\sqrt{b} + 3 = 12$

12. $\sqrt{x} = 12$

13. $\sqrt{y^2} + 2 = -2$

14. $3\sqrt{x} + 5 = 11$

15. $\sqrt{x + 5} = -4$

16. $\sqrt{m} = -7$

17. $\sqrt{2x + 2} = \sqrt{x + 3}$

18. $\sqrt{x + 6} - 4 = x$

19. $\dfrac{\sqrt{x + 8}}{3} = 4$

20. $3\sqrt{x + 2} = 12$

LESSON 76 – Direct and Inverse Variation

Our last lesson for Algebra I discusses the direct and inverse variation. They differ in that the direct variation is the **ratio** between two numbers, is always the same, and inverse variation, the **product** of the two numbers is always the same.

We shall examine direct variation with a few examples first.

Example 1:   If "y" varies directly as "x", and y = 20 when x = 30, find (a) the constant "k" and (b) find "y" when x = 45.

> Solution: Direct variation is a **ratio**.
>
> > Step 1:   Find "k".
> >
> > $$k = \frac{y}{x}$$
> > $$k = \frac{20}{30}$$
> > $$k = \frac{2}{3}$$
>
> > Step 2:   Find "y".
> >
> > $$y = kx$$
> > $$y = \frac{2}{3} \cdot 45$$
> > $$y = 30$$
>
> Solution: (a) $k = \frac{2}{3}$ and (b) y = 30

Example 2:   The shadows of two buildings vary directly as their heights at any given time. If a building 80 feet tall casts a 25-foot shadow. how tall is a building that casts a 15-foot shadow?

> Solution: This is solved by using proportions.
>
> $$\frac{\text{height of building 1}}{\text{shadow of building 1}} = \frac{\text{height of building 2}}{\text{shadow of building 2}}$$

$$\frac{80 \text{ feet}}{25 \text{ feet}} = \frac{h \text{ feet}}{15 \text{ feet}} \quad \text{cross multiply}$$

$$(25)(h) = (80)(15)$$

$$25h = 1200$$

$$h = 48$$

Solution: The height of the building is 48 feet.

Example 3: If "y" varies directly as "x" and x = 4 when y = 12, then what is "x" when y = 21?

Solution: You can use either method.

$$\frac{y}{x} = k \qquad\qquad \frac{y_1}{x_1} = \frac{y_2}{x_2}$$

$$\frac{12}{4} = k \qquad\qquad \frac{12}{4} = \frac{21}{x}$$

$$3 = k \qquad\qquad 12x = 4(21)$$

$$\qquad\qquad\qquad 12x = 84$$

$$\frac{21}{x} = 3 \qquad\qquad x = 7$$

$$3x = 21$$

$$x = 7$$

Solution: x = 7 when y = 21

Either method can be used to solve direction variations.

Now for some inverse variation examples.

Example 4: Give a formula to show how "b" varies inversely with "e", using "k" as the constant.

Solution: Inverse variation is a **product**. Remember, their products equal the constant.

$$eb = k$$

Example 5: Suppose "y" varies inversely as "x", and x = 2 when y = 1. Find (a) the constant and (b) when x = 4, the "y" is what?

Solution: (a) $xy = k$
                       $2 \cdot 1 = k$
                       $2 = k$

                (b) $xy = k$
                       $4y = 2$
                       $y = \frac{1}{2}$

Solution: (a) k = 2 and (b) $y = \frac{1}{2}$

Example 6: Electrical resistance (R) in a wire varies **directly** as the length (L) and **inversely** as the square of the diameter (D). (a) Express this variation in equation form. (b) If 4250 ft of a $\frac{5}{32}$-inch wire has a resistance of 13.6 ohms, how long would a $\frac{3}{16}$-inch wire have to be in order to have a resistance of 4.2 ohms?

Solution: (a) $R = \frac{kL}{d^2}$

                (b) $13.6 = \dfrac{4250k}{\left(\frac{5}{32}\right)^2}$

                       $k = 7.8125 \times 10^{-5}$

                       $4.2 = \dfrac{L(7.8125 \times 10^{-5})}{\left(\frac{3}{16}\right)^2}$

                       $1890 = L$

Solution: (a) $R = \frac{kL}{d^2}$ and (b) k = 7,8125 × 10^{-5} and L = 1890 feet

Solve these direct and inverse variation problems.

1. If "y" varies directly as the square of "x", so that $y = kx^2$, find "k" when y = 32 and x = 4.

2. The weight (w) of a disk varies directly as the square of the diameter (d). If a disk 4 inches in diameter weighs 4.8 pounds, find the diameter of a disk weighing 14.7 pounds.

3. If "a" varies inversely as "b" and a = 20 when b = 0.35, find "b" when a = 2.

4. If "x" and "y" vary inversely, and x = 3 when y = 8, find "y" when x = 2.

5. Suppose that "y" varies inversely as "x", and x = 5 when y = 2. Find "x" when y = 4.

6. If "y" varies directly as "x" and y = 15 when x = 20, find the constant of variation.

7. The air pressure (p) within an automobile tire varies directly as the absolute temperature (t), given in degrees Kelvin. If the air pressure in a tire is 30 pounds per square inch at 280° Kelvin, what is the pressure at 315° Kelvin?

8. Electrical resistance in a wire "R" varies directly as the length of a wire (L) and inversely as the square of the diameter (d): $R = \dfrac{kL}{d^2}$. If 4250 feet of $\frac{5}{32}$ -inch wire has a resistance of 13.6 ohms, how long would a $\frac{3}{16}$ -inch wire have to be in order to have a resistance of 4.2 ohms?

9. Identify each equation as representing direct or inversion variation.

    a. P = 1.25C

    b. $y = \dfrac{16}{x}$

10. Write an equation, using "k" as a constant, for the speed of a gear wheel (r) varies inversely as the number of teeth (n).

ANSWERS

Lesson 1
1. -9	15. -118	29. -2	43. -2	57. 30
2. 8	16. 0	30. -37	44. 6	58. 112
3. 3	17. -96	31. 6	45. 17	59. 35
4. 72	18. 39	32. -63	46. -24	60. -30
5. -9	19. 5	33. -4	47. 5	61. -9
6. -23	20. -8	34. 16	48. 5	62. -28
7. 6	21. -47	35. -4	49. -10	63. 5
8. -5	22. 22	36. 10	50. -8	64. 15
9. 36	23. 40	37. -18	51. -17	65. 4
10. -32	24. 4	38. -32	52. 8	66. 4
11. -6	25. 25	39. 11	53. -51	67. 1
12. -2	26. -14	40. 5	54. 6	68. 0
13. -16	27. -54	41. -60	55. 24	69. -3
14. -4	28. -3	42. -20	56. -2	70. -8

Lesson 3
1. 78	6. -12	11. 22	16. 1	21. 6	26. 10
2. 144	7. 84	12. 6	17. -6	22. 23	27. 5
3. 10	8. -4	13. 11	18. 4	23. -272	28. 10
4. 5	9. -1	14. -8	19. 8	24. 22	29. 5
5. -13	10. 27	15. 21	20. 3	25. -6	30. 48

Lesson 4
1. 6	5. 49	9. 48	13. -3	17. -8
2. 72	6. 3	10. 16	14. 34	18. 28
3. 4	7. 50	11. 68	15. 63	19. -2
4. 15	8. -14	12. 25	16. 22	20. 74

Lesson 5
1. 4	4. 55	7. 20	10. 3	13. 72
2. 21	5. 0	8. -39	11. 7	14. -2
3. 36	6. 24	9. -4	12. 15	15. -9

Lesson 6
1. 25	5. 61	9. 180	13. -25	17. 69
2. 31	6. -11	10. 61	14. 7	18. 25
3. -89	7. 200	11. 13	15. 12	19. 145
4. 128	8. -12	12. 31	16. 200	20. 200

Lesson 7
1. N = 6	5. N = 19	9. N = -24	13. N = 28	17. N = -4
2. N = 24	6. N = -19	10. N = 35	14. N = 60	18. N = -25
3. N = 50	7. N = 38	11. N = 3	15. N = 7	19. N = 53
4. N = 35	8. N = 25	12. N = -20	16. N = -31	20. N = -11

Lesson 8
1. x = 7	5. x = 84	9. x = 85	13. x = -3	17. x = 512
2. x = 14	6. x = -6	10. x = -4	14. x = -9	18. x = -4
3. x = 18	7. x = -5	11. x = 46	15. x = 31	19. x = 18
4. x = 11	8. x = -6	12. x = 12	16. x = -21	20. x = -70

Lesson 9

1. x = 4	13. x = 15	25. x = 7	37. x = 14	49. x = 2
2. x = 3	14. x = -32	26. x = -8	38. x = 6	50. x = 5
3. x = 5	15. x = 14	27. x = 5	39. x = 2	51. x = -4
4. x = 7	16. x = 6	28. x = 10	40. x = 1.5	52. x = -7
5. x = -18	17. x = 6	29. x = -12	41. x = 3	53. x = 4
6. x = 10.88	18. x – 8	30. x = 5	42. x = -8	54. x = -9
7. x = 4.6	19. x = 5	31. x = -3	43. x = -2	55. x = -9
8. x = 8.32	20. x = -3	32. x = -4	44. x = 2	56. x = 3
9. x = 17	21. x = -6	33. x = -7	45. x = 7	57. x = 6
10. x = 12	22. x = 2	34. x = -8	46. x = -3	58. x = 3
11. x = 3.8	23. x = -20	35. x = 7	47. x = 4	59. x = -5
12. x = 60	24. x = 2	36. x = 14	48. x = 1.33	60. x = -9

Lesson 12

1. x = -6.4	5. x = 4	9. x = 4	13. x = 6	17. x = 4
2. x = -3	6. x = -2.7	10. x = -2	14. x = 172.8	18. x = -3
3. x = 0.23	7. x = -2	11. x = -5.3	15. x = -2.1	19. x = -47.31
4. x = -4.6	8. x = 3.76	12. x = -0.375	16. x = 6.3	20. x = -2

Lesson 13

1. x = 12	10. x = 63	19. x = 10	28. N = -8	37. N = 16
2. $x = 4\frac{1}{5}$	11. $x = -\frac{1}{24}$	20. $x = \frac{1}{2}$	29. x = 7	38. x = 10
3. $x = \frac{53}{62}$	12. x = -60	21. N = 3	30. N = 9	39. $N = 5\frac{4}{7}$
4. x = 3	13. x = 4	22. N = 7.6	31. x = 2	40. x = -12
5. x = 30	14. x = -18	23. N = 1	32. $x = 8\frac{1}{3}$	41. N = 15
6. x = -9	15. x = 24	24. N = 20	33. x = 64	42. x = -40
7. x = 24	16. $x = -1\frac{1}{2}$	25. x = 8	34. x = 16	43. A = 2
8. x = 3	17. $x = 1\frac{3}{5}$	26. N = 4	35. x = 20	44. B = 48
9. $x = 1\frac{1}{4}$	18. x = -36	27. x = 6	36. N = -16	45. m = 1

Lesson 15

1. $r = \dfrac{i}{pt}$	7. $g = \dfrac{v - V}{t}$	13. $d = \dfrac{L - a}{n - 1}$	19. $p = A - i$
2. $b = \dfrac{2A}{h}$	8. $r = \dfrac{A - p}{pt}$	14. $v = \dfrac{P}{F}$	20. $D = \dfrac{dr}{R}$
3. $H = \dfrac{V}{LW}$	9. $L = \dfrac{1}{2}(P - 2W)$	15. $I = \dfrac{E}{R + r}$	21. $R = \dfrac{P - TOP}{Q}$
4. $L = \dfrac{A}{W}$	10. $h = \dfrac{S - 2\pi r^2}{2\pi r}$	16. $B = 90 - A$	22. $W = \dfrac{3}{2}(2H - 9)$
5. $c = s - g$	11. $n = \dfrac{s + 360}{180}$	17. $s = \sqrt{A}$	23. $x = \dfrac{z - 2y}{y}$
6. $h = \dfrac{3V}{b}$	12. $A = \dfrac{p^2}{16}$	18. $S = \dfrac{Ndtt}{12}$	24. $b = \dfrac{d(1 - ac)}{ac}$

Lesson 18

1. a. $y = 3$

   b. $x = 1\frac{3}{4}$

   c. $y = 1$

   d. $x = -\frac{3}{4}$

2. a. $x = 7\frac{1}{2}$

   b. $y = -2\frac{2}{3}$

   c. $x = 6$

   d. $y = -6$

3. a. no, yes

   b. yes, yes

   c. no, no

   d. yes, no

Lesson 20

1. parallel
2. parallel
3. intersect but not perpendicular
4. perpendicular
5. intersect but not perpendicular
6. parallel
7. intersect but not perpendicular
8. coincide
9. perpendicular
10. intersect but not perpendicular
11. parallel
12. coincide

Lesson 21

1. $\frac{6}{5}$
2. -1
3. $-\frac{3}{2}$

4. -3
5. $\frac{1}{6}$
6. $\frac{1}{5}$

7. $\frac{2}{7}$
8. $\frac{145}{128}$
9. 1

10. 1
11. $\frac{13}{2}$
12. $-\frac{8}{5}$

13. -1
14. $\frac{3}{8}$
15. 1

16. 2
17. $-\frac{3}{4}$
18. $-\frac{9}{2}$

19. -1
20. $-\frac{2}{3}$

Lesson 22

1. $2x - y = -2$

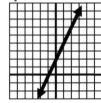

3.

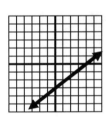

5.

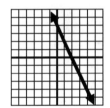

2. $x - y = 2$

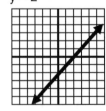

4. $8x + 5y = 40$, negative

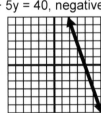

6. intersecting

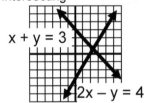

$x + y = 3$

$2x - y = 4$

Lesson 23

1. zeros: $(0, -2)$, $(4, 0)$
   slope: $\frac{1}{2}$
   y-intercept: -2

2. zeros: $(0, \frac{3}{2})$, $(-6, 0)$
   slope: $\frac{1}{4}$
   y-intercept: $\frac{3}{2}$

3. zeros: $(0, 0)$, $(0, 0)$
   slope: 4
   y-intercept: 0

4. zeros: $(0, 8)$, $(4, 0)$
   slope: -2
   y-intercept: 8

5. zeros: $(0, -\frac{5}{3})$, $(-\frac{5}{2}, 0)$
   slope: $-\frac{2}{3}$
   y-intercept: $-\frac{5}{3}$

6. zeros: $(0, 0)$, $(0, 0)$
   slope: -1
   y-intercept: 0

7. zeros: $(0, 9)$, $(18, 0)$
   slope: $-\frac{1}{2}$
   y-intercept: 9

8. zeros: $(0, 12)$, $(4, 0)$
   slope: -3
   y-intercept: 12

9. zeros: $(0, 2)$, $(-3, 0)$
   slope: $\frac{2}{3}$
   y-intercept: 2

10. zeros: $(0, -10)$, $(\frac{10}{3}, 0)$
    slope: 3
    y-intercept: -10

11. zeros: $(0, 0)$, $(0, 0)$
    slope: $\frac{1}{4}$
    y-intercept: 0

12. zeros: $(0, 5)$, $(\frac{5}{4}, 0)$
    slope: -4
    y-intercept: 5

Lesson 27

1. $2x - y = -6$
2. $4x + 7y = 26$
3. $3x - 2y = -5$
4. $x = -3$
5. $5x - 8y = -2$
6. $2x + 3y = -2$
7. $y = -5$
8. $3x - y = 0$
9. $3x + 4y = -8$
10. $4x + 3y = 1$

Lesson 28

1.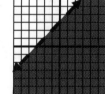
2.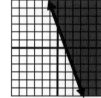
3.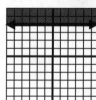
4.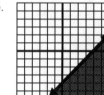
5.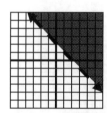
6.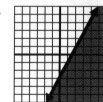
7.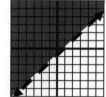
8.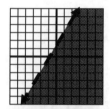
9.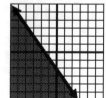

Lesson 30

1. $12x^3 - 15x^2 + 18x$
2. $-x^5 + 4x^4 + 3x^3 - 7x^2$
3. $6x^3 + 24x^2 + 36x$
4. $-a^3 + a^2b + 5ab^2$
5. $abc^2 - 3abc + 4ab$
6. $36x^2 - 6x + 1$
7. $8x^2 + 3x - 20$
8. $100y^3 - 60y^2 - 15$
9. $-32e^4 + 16e^3 - 8e^2 - 24e$
10. $-9f^3 + 36f^2 - 3f$
11. $15x^8z^4 + 10x^5z^6 - 20x^4z^7$
12. $-10a^4c^2 + 15a^3c^3 + 5a^2c^5$
13. $16y^{10}$
14. $-100a^6b^9$
15. $2a^3b^3 + 4a^5b^3 - 3a^2b^7$

Lesson 31
1. $2x^2 - 12x - 6$
2. $7n^2 - 4n - 4$
3. $4a^3 - 8a^2 + 14a - 10$
4. $-6y^3 + 12y^2 - 9y + 1$
5. $4x^2 - 27x + 17$

6. $2a^2 + 6a + 2$
7. $x^2 - 18x - 17$
8. $4x^3 + 7x^2 + x - 14$
9. $8x^3 - 16x^2 + 2x + 2$
10. $2a^3 + 2a^2 + a - 14$

11. $2x^2 + 5x - 7$
12. $-9m^2 + mn + n^2$
13. $4x^2 - x - 11$
14. $2a^2 + 3a - 14$
15. $6x^2 - 18x - 8$

16. $-4x^3 + x^2 - 3x + 1$
17. $-x - 5y$
18. $2ab^2 - 6a^2b^2 + a^2b - ab^3$
19. $5n^2 - 3n - 11$
20. $8xy^2 - 4y^3 + 6$

Lesson 32
1. $10x^2 - 19x - 15$
2. $-2a^2 - 7ab - 3b^2$
3. $16a^2 + 40ac + 25c^2$
4. $-2c^2 + 3cd + 9d^2$
5. $42x^2 - 29xy - 5y^2$

6. $3c^2 - 5cd - 2d^2$
7. $10r^2 + 19rs + 6s^2$
8. $e^2 - f^2$
9. $-20x^2 - 9x + 18$
10. $9x^2 - 42xy + 49y^2$

11. $6x^4 - x^2 - 35$
12. $x^2y^4 - z^2$
13. $-15a^2 - 13a + 6$
14. $4b^6 + 12b^3 + 9$
15. $8a^2 - 2a - 21$

16. $4b^2 + 3b - 27$
17. $21x^2 + xy - 2y^2$
18. $60a^2 + 41a - 3$
19. $30x^2 - 7xy - 15y^2$
20. $12y^2 + 7yz - 10z^2$

Lesson 33
1. $y^3 - 2y^2 - 11y + 12$
2. $2a^4 - 3a^2 - 8a^2 + 14a - 3$
3. $x^3 + 10x^2 + 16x - 35$
4. $x^3 - 9x^2 + 9x + 54$
5. $6b^3 - 34b^2 + 49b - 15$
6. $4x^3 - 29x^2 + 33x - 18$
7. $2c^3 - 9c^2 + 18c - 20$

8. $6a^3 - a^2 + 24a + 48$
9. $12y^3 - 25y^2 - 25y + 42$
10. $4z^3 + 7z^2 - 31z + 20$
11. $18a^2 + 9a - 20$
12. $6b^3 - 7b^2 - 5b + 3$
13. $6x^3 + 29x^2 + 23x - 30$
14. $2a^3 - 5a^2 + a + 2$

15. $27a^3 - 108a^2 + 144a - 64$
16. $3d^3 + 14d^2 + d - 2$
17. $-2a^3 + 2a^2 + 12a$
18. $3y^4 - 2y^3 + 4y^2 - 2y + 1$
19. $x^4 - x^3 - 8x^2 + 11x - 3$
20. $a^4 + 2a^3b - 11a^2b^2 - 12ab^3 + 36b^3$

Lesson 34
1. $12x^3 - 9x^2 + 27x - 3$

2. $4x^3 - 3x^2 - 6x + 10$

3. $4x^2 - 6x + 10 + \dfrac{8}{x}$

4. $3a^2b^2c^2 - 5abc + 2$

5. $6x^2 - 2x + \dfrac{5}{2} - \dfrac{4}{x}$

6. $6a^3 + 5a^2 - 8a + 3 - \dfrac{4}{a}$

7. $9a^3 + 6a^2 - 5a + 10$

8. $4b^3 - 3b^2 + 6b - 2 + \dfrac{5}{b}$

9. $a^2 + 2ab - 3b^2$

10. $cd + \dfrac{1}{d} - \dfrac{1}{c}$

11. $-4d^3 + 3cd + 2$

12. $-y^2 - 3y + 2$

13. $1 - 2a - 3a^2 + 6a^3$

14. $-5x^3y^2 + 3xy^3 - 8y^4$

15. $3x^2y - x + 2 - 5xy$

16. $-5a^3 + 4a^2 - 8a - 12 + \dfrac{14}{a}$

17. $\dfrac{5x^2}{y} + 7x - 8y + \dfrac{3y^2}{x}$

18. $-6x^2z + 8x^3yz^3$

19. $x^2 + 4 - 2x - \dfrac{8}{x}$

20. $-3x^2 + 4x - 5 - \dfrac{2}{x}$

Lesson 35
1. $x^2 - 5x + 13 + \dfrac{-27}{x + 2}$

2. $x^2 + 4x + 4$

3. $x^2 + 7x + 7 + \dfrac{17}{x - 2}$

4. $x^2 + 9x + 39 + \dfrac{125}{x - 3}$

5. $x - 4 + \dfrac{-4}{2x + 1}$

6. $x^2 - x + 1 + \dfrac{-2}{x + 1}$

7. $3x^2 - 2x + 3 + \dfrac{-4}{3x + 2}$

8. $2x^3 + 3x^2 + 2x + 3 + \dfrac{16}{2x - 3}$

9. $4x^2 - 4x + 1$

10. $4x^2 - 8x + 7 + \dfrac{-8}{2x + 1}$

Lesson 37
1. $5x(2x + 1)$
2. $5a^2(3a + 2b^2 - b)$
3. $4t(15t^3 - at + 3)$
4. $15x^2y(2y + 3 - 5y^2)$
5. $3x(3x^3 - 6x^2 + 4x - 10)$
6. $10h(12h^4 + 10h^3 + 5h^2 + 1)$
7. $xy(6x^4 - 15x^3y + 20x^2y^2 + 6y^4)$
8. $7a^2(a^4 + 3a^3b^2 + 3b^5 + a^2b^3)$
9. $21x^4y^3(3x^2y^2z^4 - 5xyz^3 + 1)$
10. $21x^2y^2(4x^6y^3 + 5x - 3y)$
11. $3r^2s^2t^2(7st^2 + 10r + 2s^2t^3 - 6r^2t^2)$
12. $7x^2y^2z^2(2xyz^2 - 4y + 5x^3z - 7y^2z^3)$
13. $5a^2bc^2(3a + 5b - 6a^2b^2c^2 + 12abc^2)$
14. $6L^2m^2n^3(3mn - 6Lm + 4L^2m^2n^2 + 8L)$
15. $4(2x^3 - 4x^2 + 11x - 6)$
16. $3ab(7ab + 11b^2 - 21a^2 + 5)$
17. $4mn(5m^2n^2 - 7m + 4n)$
18. $4xy(3xy - 4x^2 + 5y - 8x^3y^2)$
19. $11z^2(11z^2 + 3 - 6z - 9z^3)$
20. $2c^4(c^2 + 4c - 21)$

Lesson 38
1. $(5c + 4d)(25c^2 - 20cd + 16d^2)$
2. $(1 + 13x^2)(1 - 13x^2)$
3. $(2x + 1)(2x - 1)(4x^2 + 2x + 1)(4x^2 - 2x + 1)$
4. $3x(x + 5)(x - 5)$
5. $(5t^3 + 12)(5t^3 - 12)$
6. $(3a + \frac{1}{3})(3a - \frac{1}{3})$
7. $6x + 9 = 3(2x + 3)$
8. $(5a + 8)(25a^2 - 40a + 64)$
9. $3a(3a + 11b)(3a - 11b)$
10. $4a$
11. $3x(3x + 11y)(3x - 11y)$
12. $x^4 - 8x^2 = x^2(x^2 - 8)$

Lesson 39
1. $(y^2 - 3)(y + 2)$
2. $(3a - 1)(3b + 4)$
3. $(x^2 + 9)(x + 1)$
4. $(2c - 5d)(c - 4)$
5. $(2x - 3)(y - 4)$
6. $(3a + 2b)(6a - c)$
7. $(x + 3y)(5x - 2z)$
8. $(x - 2)(y + 1)(y - 1)$
9. $(5f^2 - 4)(2f + 3)$
10. $(y + 1)(y + 3)(y - 3)$
11. $(a - c)(2x + y)$
12. $(a + c)(b + 2)(b - 2)$
13. $(x - 1)(y - 1)$
14. $6a(a + 3)(b - 4)$

Lesson 40
1. $-4a$
2. forgot the CMF (3k) in the answer
3. $25(x^2 + 3y^3)(x^2 - 3y^3)$
4. $(4c - d^2)(4c^2 - d)$
5. $2x$
6. $(4 + x - y)(4 - x + y)$
7. $x(x + 3)(x - 3)$
8. true
9. $9(2x + 3y)(2x - 3y)$
10. a. 27
    b. $27(1 - 2e)(1 + 2e + 4e^2)$
11. $-56st$
12. $(a + 2b)(a - 7)$
13. $(x - 1)(3y - 4)$ or $(4 - 3y)(1 - x)$
14. $5y(x + 5y)(x - 5y)$
15. a. $(x + 1)(x - 1)(x^4 + x^2 + 1)$
    b. $(x + 1)(x - 1)(x^2 + x + 1)(x^2 - x + 1)$

Lesson 41
1. $(x + 3)(x - 13)$
2. $(y - 5)(y - 19)$
3. $(y + 16)(y + 1)$
4. $(t - 43)(t - 1)$
5. $(c - 1)(c - 2)$
6. $(x + 1)(x - 19)$
7. $x(x + 5)(x + 3)$
8. $3(a - 9)(a - 2)$
9. $(a + 19)(a + 7)$
10. $(r + 13)(r + 2)$
11. $(a + 31)(a - 2)$
12. $(h - 3)(h - 3)$
13. $x(x - 17)(x - 1)$
14. $-2(x + 7)(x - 5)$
15. $(x - 16)(x + 1)$
16. $(w + 48)(w + 3)$
17. $(a - 14)(a - 2)$
18. $(b + 9)(b + 2)$
19. $(k - 5)(k - 5)$
20. $-x(x - 3)(x - 1)$

Lesson 42
1. $(3x + 2)(x + 2)$
2. $(3x - 2)(x - 1)$
3. $(5x - 12)(x + 1)$
4. $(5x + 4)(x + 3)$
5. $(3x + 1)(x - 2)$
6. $(2x + 1)(3x - 5)$
7. $(3x + 2)(2x + 5)$
8. $(4x + 3)(4x + 3)$
9. $(x - 3)(8x - 3)$
10. $(3x - 10)(2x - 1)$
11. $(3x + 2)(2x - 3)$
12. $(7x - 8)(3x + 1)$
13. $(x + 1)(4x + 3)$
14. $(7x + 4)(4x - 1)$
15. $2(3x + 5)(x + 1)$
16. $9x(x + 1)(x + 1)$
17. $2y(7x + 4)(2x - 1)$
18. $6x(2x + 3)(x - 1)$
19. $2(7x + 4y)(x - y)$
20. $x^2y(5x + 4y)(5x + 4y)$

Lesson 43

1. $2a^4(a-3)(a+7)$
2. $(3x-2)(5x-3)$
3. $(7+a)(1+a)$
4. $2x(2x+3)(3x-2)$
5. $(-1)(2x-3)(x+4)$
6. $(x+3)(x+2)$
7. $a(n-2)(n-4)$
8. $(x+1)(x-1)(y+3)(y-3)$
9. $25y^2(y+2)(y-2)$
10. $3x(5x+1)(2x+3)$
11. $(-3)(2r-s)^2$ or $(-3)(s-2r)^2$
12. $(x-2)(x+1)(x-1)$
13. $3(15x+y)(x-4y)$
14. $(x-1)(x-2)(x+2)$
15. $(a+2)(a+3)(a-3)$
16. $(x+y-5)(x-y+1)$
17. $(x+1)(x-2)$
18. $-2(x+17)(x-5)$
19. $2(x^2+9)(x+3)(x-3)$
20. $(3x-2)(x+4)$

Lesson 45

1. $\{0, 4\}$
2. $\{-4, \frac{1}{2}\}$
3. $\{-3\}$
4. $\{-2, 5\}$
5. $\{-\frac{3}{2}, 0\}$
6. $\{-4, 3\}$
7. $\{-\frac{9}{2}, \frac{8}{3}\}$
8. $\{1, 9\}$
9. $\{-\frac{1}{2}, \frac{5}{2}\}$
10. $\{-\frac{1}{3}, \frac{1}{2}\}$
11. $\{-8, 3\}$
12. $\{-2, 9\}$
13. $\{-3, \frac{2}{5}\}$
14. $\{-\frac{1}{3}, \frac{1}{2}\}$
15. $\{-1, 1\}$
16. $\{\frac{1}{4}, 7\}$
17. $\{-2, \frac{1}{3}\}$
18. $\{-7, 6\}$
19. $\{0, 16\}$
20. $\{-5, -3\}$

Lesson 46

1. 15
2. $2\sqrt{10}$
3. $2\sqrt{30}$
4. $8\sqrt{2}$
5. $30\sqrt{2}$
6. 26
7. $27\sqrt{10}$
8. 18
9. $60\sqrt{2}$
10. $18\sqrt{5}$
11. $50\sqrt{3}$
12. $24\sqrt{3}$
13. $8\sqrt{2}$
14. $12\sqrt{6}$
15. 85
16. -4
17. 12
18. $2\sqrt{3}$
19. $20\sqrt{5}$
20. $-20\sqrt{3}$
21. $-4\sqrt{6}$
22. $10\sqrt{3}$
23. $15\sqrt{3}$
24. $18\sqrt{7}$
25. $50\sqrt{2}$
26. $12\sqrt{2}$
27. $30\sqrt{6}$
28. -140
29. $30\sqrt{5}$
30. $28\sqrt{2}$
31. $64\sqrt{5}$
32. -33
33. $60\sqrt{2}$
34. $16\sqrt{14}$
35. $12\sqrt{5}$
36. $24\sqrt{2}$
37. $-8\sqrt{6}$
38. $25\sqrt{5}$
39. $96\sqrt{5}$
40. $-6\sqrt{15}$
41. 25
42. $66\sqrt{2}$
43. $-14\sqrt{7}$
44. $108\sqrt{5}$
45. $100\sqrt{5}$

Lesson 47

1. $x = 1 \pm \sqrt{21}$
2. $z = 3 \pm 4\sqrt{21}$
3. $a = -\frac{1}{2} \pm \frac{\sqrt{21}}{2}$
4. $x = -6 \pm \sqrt{38}$
5. $t = 2 \pm \sqrt{7}$
6. $d = -7 \pm 2\sqrt{11}$
7. $x = -4 \pm \sqrt{26}$
8. $c = -22, 6$
9. $t = -3 \pm 3\sqrt{2}$
10. $a = -37, 31$
11. $x = -30, 2$
12. $a = -\frac{1}{2}, -2\frac{1}{2}$

Lesson 48

1. $a = -2 \pm \sqrt{10}$
2. $x = \frac{-9 \pm \sqrt{41}}{20}$
3. $y = \frac{25 \pm 3\sqrt{105}}{8}$
4. $y = \frac{3 \pm 2\sqrt{3}}{2}$
5. $x = \frac{-1 \pm \sqrt{7}}{3}$
6. $x = -1 \pm \frac{\sqrt{7}}{2}$
7. $a = \frac{7 \pm \sqrt{65}}{2}$
8. $y = \frac{-3 \pm \sqrt{17}}{2}$
9. $n = \frac{3 \pm \sqrt{5}}{2}$
10. $x = -2, 5$
11. $s = \frac{-7 \pm \sqrt{149}}{10}$
12. $x = -21, 20$

Lesson 49

1. $x = -\frac{1}{2}, 4$
2. $x = \frac{1}{3}, 4$
3. $a = -3, 4$
4. $x = -\frac{5}{2}, \frac{3}{8}$
5. $n = \frac{3 \pm \sqrt{13}}{2}$
6. $y = \frac{3 \pm \sqrt{13}}{2}$
7. $y = -\frac{5}{8}, \frac{7}{6}$
8. $a = 5 \pm \sqrt{35}$
9. $x = 2, 5$
10. $x = -\frac{3}{2}, 0$
11. $y = -\frac{6}{7}, \frac{5}{6}$
12. $y = -1, 3$
13. $a = \frac{-3 \pm \sqrt{7}}{2}$
14. $y = -1$

163

Lesson 50

1. a = 5, b = 1
2. c = 3, d = -2
3. x = 3, y = -3
4. x = 9, y = 5

5. x = 1, y = 2
6. x = -1, y = 2
7. x = -1, y = 2
8. x = 13, y = -2

9. x = 2, y = -4
10. x = 8, y = 0
11. x = 7, y = 2

12. x = 2, y = -3
13. x = $\frac{1}{4}$, y = $\frac{1}{2}$
14. x = -4, y = 3

Lesson 51

1. m = $\frac{9}{2}$, n = $\frac{1}{4}$
2. a = 2, b = 3
3. a = 4, b = 6
4. x = 2, y = 0

5. x = $\frac{1}{3}$, y = 1
6. a = 6, b = -3
7. x = $\frac{1}{2}$, y = $\frac{1}{2}$
8. x = 7, y = -1

9. x = 2, y = 6
10. x = 21, y = 3
11. x = 1, y = 1
12. x = 2, y = -$\frac{1}{3}$

13. x = 6, y = 1
14. x = 3, y = -1
15. x = -1, y = 2
16. x = -$\frac{5}{7}$, y = $\frac{10}{7}$

Lesson 53

1. a = 3, y = 5
2. e = 7, f = 1
3. x = 5, y = -2
4. x = 20, y = 32

5. p = 9, q = 12
6. m = 14, n = 10
7. x = 4, y = 2
8. x = 2, y = 0

9. a = 4, b = 3
10. x = 4, y = $\frac{4}{5}$
11. x = 3, y = 4
12. x = 0, y = 1

13. t = 7, u = 4
14. c = -4, d = -6
15. x = 2, y = -1
16. r = 90, s = 72, t = 18

Lesson 54

1. a. 23 mph
   b. 21 miles
2. 40 minutes
3. 50 mph
4. 4 miles

5. a. 215 miles
   b. 215 miles
6. 2:30 P.M.
7. a. west: 800 mph, east: 860 mph
   b. 150 miles

8. 3 miles in 18 minutes
9. 5 P.M.
10. 6 miles
11. car: 54 mph, boat: 24 mph
12. 2:30 P.M.

Lesson 55

1. 17 quarters, 33 dimes
2. 9 dimes, 15 nickels
3. $3.45
4. 10 pennies, 6 nickels, 7 dimes

5. 15 nickels, 18 quarters
6. 17 nickels worth 85¢
   10 dimes worth $1
   15 quarters worth $3.75

7. 18 quarters, 6 half-dollars
8. 72 quarters, 98 dimes
9. 5 quarters, 45 nickels

Lesson 56

1. 48
2. 124
3. 27
4. 96
5. 38
6. 79
7. 72
8. 360
9. 342
10. 51
11. 85
12. 17

Lesson 57

1. 5 notebooks
2. 5 hours
3. 48 stamps
4. 8 pennants
5. corn: 55¢
   peas: 75¢
6. 900 adults
   600 students
7. plumber: $65
   apprentice: $50

Lesson 58

1. Arnie: 20, Andy: 7
2. Peter: 7, Bart: 1
3. Mack: 26, Dave: 25
4. Sue: 17$\frac{2}{3}$, dog: $\frac{1}{3}$

5. Alan: 18, Lynda: 14
6. Gary: 14, Leslie: 8
7. Matilda: 16, Matty: 6
8. Mary: 34, Bob: 26

9. Tyler McCloud: 1882
   Pittsford: 1942
10. 22 years old
11. Alex: 9, Jack: 12

Lesson 59

1. apples: 8 lbs, apricots: 12 lbs
2. 36% acid
3. 50 grams of salt
4. $3 per pound

5. 25 grams of water
6. 2 pounds of salt
7. 4.8 L of water
   3.2 L of acid

8. cashews: 4 lbs, peanuts: 6 lbs
9. 200 qt of 1% buttermilk
10. 8 kg of water

Lesson 60

1. $13\frac{1}{3}$ minutes
2. 30 minutes
3. 12 hours
4. 2400 seconds = 40 minutes
5. 18 days
6. 2 hours
7. $\frac{3}{5}$ hour = 36 minutes
8. $\frac{2}{5}$ hour = 24 minutes
9. 30 minutes
10. 6 hours

Lesson 61

1. $3\frac{1}{8}$ years
2. $8.13
3. $180
4. stocks: $1600, bonds: $4400
5. $1440
6. $12,000
7. 9%
8. 12%: $24,000
   10.5%: $18,000

Lesson 62

1. 22
2. 7, 9, 11
3. 17, 18, 19, 20
4. -58, -57, -56
5. 19, 21, 23
6. length: 25 inches
   width: 23 inches
7. 16, 17
8. 18, 20
9. 15, 17
10. 63, 65, 67
11. 7, 9, 11, 13
12. 14, 16, 18
13. 5, 6, 7

Lesson 63

1. length: 12 feet
2. 18, 19, 20
3. $1\frac{1}{3}$ hours
4. 84
5. 8, 10, 12
6. 12, 13, 14, 15, 16, 17
7. 2
8. 10
9. 52

Lesson 64

1. $2160
2. 6.25
3. 20%
4. 20%
5. 24%
6. 25%
7. $2000
8. $6.37
9. $1000
10. 2 minutes
11. 20%
12. $5400
13. 40
14. $12\frac{1}{2}$%
15. 144

Lesson 65

1. 9 in.^{2}
2. length: 14.5 inches
   width: 9.5 inches
3. 25 ft by 40 ft
4. 5 inches
5. 7 inches
6. $11\frac{1}{2}$ ft, $8\frac{1}{2}$ ft
7. length: 40 units
   width: 16 units
8. 43°, 94°
9. 84°, 96°
10. less than

Lesson 66

1. 11 and 12
   -11 and -12
2. 6 hours
3. 33.33% or $33\frac{1}{3}$%
4. 250%
5. 25%
6. 8 inches each side
7. 9 in., 12 in., 15 in.
8. 16°, 65°, 99°
9. 39
10. 32 nickels, 47 dimes
11. 2

Lesson 67

1. a. no
   b. yes
   c. no
   d. yes
   e. yes
2. yes
3. yes
4. a. 23
   b. 8
   c. -1
   d. -4

4. e. -1
   f. $3a^2 - 4$
   g. $3b^2 - 4$
   h. $3y^2 - 4$
   i. $27x^2 - 4$
   j. $3c^4 - 4$
5. b, d, f
6. a. i. 69
      ii. $\frac{31}{10}$
      iii. $a^6 + a^4 - 3a^2 + 4$
   b. i. 45

6. b. ii. $\frac{39}{24} = \frac{13}{8}$
      iii. $3a^4 + 12$
   c. i. -12
      ii. $\frac{17}{13}$
      iii. $-4a^2 - 5$
   d. i. 102
      ii. $\frac{63}{29}$
      iii. $8a^4 - 6a^2 + 9$
   e. i. 15
      ii. $\frac{8}{3}$
      iii. $5a^2 - 7$

Lesson 68

1. a. 10
   b. -3
   c. 21

1. d. $\frac{5}{3}$
   e. 45
   f. $3d^2 + 1$

1. g. -8
   h. 30

1. i. 17
   j. -3

2. a. yes   b. yes   c. no   d. no   e. yes   f. no   g. yes   h. no

Lesson 69

1.   vertex: (0,0)
     axis of symmetry: x = 0

x	-2	-1	0	1	2
y	16	4	0	4	16

2.   vertex: (0, 5)
     axis of symmetry: x = 0

x	-2	-1	0	1	2
y	-7	2	5	2	-7

3.   vertex: (0, -5)
     axis of symmetry: x = 0

x	-2	-1	0	1	2
y	-4	$-4\frac{3}{4}$	-5	$-4\frac{3}{4}$	-4

4.   vertex: (0, 6)
     axis of symmetry: x = 0

x	-2	-1	0	1	2
y	-2	4	6	4	-2

5.   vertex: (0, -2)
     axis of symmetry: x = 0

x	-2	-1	0	1	2
y	10	1	-2	1	10

6.   vertex: (0, 3)
     axis of symmetry: x = 0

x	-2	-1	0	1	2
y	0	$2\frac{1}{4}$	3	$2\frac{1}{4}$	0

7.   vertex: (0, 0)
     axis of symmetry: x = 0

x	-2	-1	0	1	2
y	-4	-1	0	-1	-4

8.   vertex: (0, 4)
     axis of symmetry: x = 0

x	-2	-1	0	1	2
y	-4	2	4	2	-4

Lesson 71

1. domain: all real numbers
    range: y ≥ 0
    vertex: (-2, 0)
    minimum point
    axis of symmetry: x = -2

x	-3	-2	-1	0	1
y	1	0	1	4	9

2. domain: all real numbers
    range: y ≤ -2
    vertex: (-1, -2)
    maximum point
    axis of symmetry: x = -1

x	-3	-2	-1	0	1
y	-6	-3	-2	-3	-6

3. domain: all real numbers
    range: y ≥ 0
    vertex: (3, 0)
    minimum point
    axis of symmetry: x = 3

x	-2	-1	0	1	2
y	25	16	9	4	1

4. domain: all real numbers
    range: y ≥ -1
    vertex: (2, -1)
    minimum point
    axis of symmetry: x = 2

x	-1	0	1	2	3
y	26	11	2	-1	2

5. domain: all real numbers
    range: y ≤ 1
    vertex: (1, 1)
    maximum point
    axis of symmetry: x = 1

x	-2	-1	0	1	2
y	-17	-7	-1	1	-1

6. domain: all real numbers
    range: y ≥ 2
    vertex: (4, 2)
    minimum point
    axis of symmetry: x = 4

x	2	3	4	5	6
y	6	3	2	3	6

7. domain: all real numbers
    range: y ≥ -5
    vertex: (-3, -5)
    minimum point
    axis of symmetry: x = -3

x	-4	-3	-2	-1	0
y	-3	-5	-3	3	13

8. domain: all real numbers
    range: y ≤ 3
    vertex: (-2, 3)
    maximum point
    axis of symmetry: x = -2

x	-3	-2	-1	0	1
y	2	3	2	-1	-6

Lesson 72

	disc. value	# of roots	roots real?	rational/irrational
1.	1	2	yes	rational
2.	80	2	yes	irrational
3.	25	2	yes	rational
4.	-44	2	no	irrational
5.	0	1	yes	rational
6.	0	1	yes	rational
7.	-204	2	no	irrational
8.	-768	2	no	irrational
9.	4	2	yes	rational
10.	0	1	yes	rational
11.	33	2	yes	irrational
12.	-12	2	no	irrational
13.	16	2	yes	rational
14.	13	2	yes	irrational
15.	0	1	yes	rational
16.	4	2	yes	rational

Lesson 73

1. 56 yards
2. 21 feet
3. 12 feet
4. 192 ft^2
5. 75 meters
6. 25 feet
7. $5\sqrt{2}$
8. yes
9. 25

Lesson 74

1. P = 24, A = 24
2. A = 144 square units
   other points: (7, 15), (-5, 15)
   diagonal: $12\sqrt{2}$ units
3. 43.75 m^2
4. 24 units
5. $10 + 2\sqrt{13} + 2\sqrt{10} + 8\sqrt{2}$
6. $2\sqrt{41}$
7. (0, 6), (6, 0), (6, 6)
8. (1, 1) and (5, 2) = $\sqrt{17}$
   (5, 2) and (4, -2) = $\sqrt{17}$
   isosceles triangle has 2 equal sides
9. (-2, -2)

Lesson 75

1. b = 5
2. e = 36
3. b = 2
4. b = 1
5. w = -11, 11
6. x = 5
7. c = 8
8. x = 36
9. no solution
10. no solution
11. b = 9
12. x = 144
13. no solution
14. x = 4
15. no solution
16. no solution
17. x = 1
18. x = -2
19. x = 136
20. x = 14

Lesson 76

1. k = 2
2. diameter: $12\frac{1}{4}$ inches
3. b = 3.5
4. y = 12
5. $x = \frac{5}{2} = 2.5$
6. $k = \frac{3}{4}$
7. 33.75 per in.^{2}
8. 1890 feet
9. a. direct variation
   b. inverse variation
10. nr = k